St. Maarten, Saba, and St. Eustatius

Jerry Schnabel and Susan L. Swygert

Pisces Books™
A division of Gulf Publishing Company
Houston, Texas

ACKNOWLEDGMENTS

The authors very much appreciate the assistance of the St. Maarten, Saba, and St. Eustatius Tourist Bureaus, the Great Bay Beach Hotel, Scout's Place, Juliana's, the Captain's Quarters, the Old Gin House, Ocean Explorers Dive Center, Tradewinds Dive Center, Saba Deep, Sea Saba, and Dive Statia. Personal thanks are extended to Cornelius de Weever; Glen Holm; Maxine and Althea; John May; Leroy French; Tom and Adrienne; Mike Meyers; Lou and Joan Bourque; John Magor; Mike, Judy, and Kim Brown; Jim Hilgers; Susan Walker White; and Tom van't Hof.

Photos by Jerry Schnabel and Susan L. Swygert. Contributing photographers: Jim Hilgers, Joan Bourque, and John Magor.

Pisces Books
A division of Gulf Publishing Company
P.O. Box 2608, Houston, Texas 77252-2608

Library of Congress Cataloging-in-Publication Data

Schnabel, Jerry.
  Diving and snorkeling guide to St. Maarten, Saba, and St. Eustatius / Jerry Schnabel and Susan L. Swygert.
       p. cm.
    Includes index.
    ISBN 1-55992-066-1
    1. Skin diving—Netherlands Antilles—Windward Islands—Guidebooks. 2. Scuba diving—Netherlands Antilles—Windward Islands—Guidebooks. 3. Windward Islands (Netherlands Antilles)—Guidebooks. I. Title.
GV840.S78S345   1994
797.2′3′0972984—dc20   94-8698
                                                      CIP

Pisces Books is a trademark of Gulf Publishing Company

Printed in Hong Kong

10 9 8 7 6 5 4 3 2 1

Publisher's note: At the time of publication of this book, all the information was determined to be as accurate as possible. However, when you use this guide, new construction may have changed land reference points, weather may have altered reef configurations, and some businesses may no longer be in operation. Your assistance in keeping future editions up-to-date will be greatly appreciated.

Also, please pay particular attention to the diver rating system in this book. Know your limits!

Table of Contents

How to Use This Guide

The unique dive sites of St. Maarten, Saba, and St. Eustatius are somewhat alike in that they require diving from a boat. There are many excellent snorkeling sites from certain shore locations which are discussed in the dive chapters as well. This guidebook describes in detail the most popular snorkeling and dive sites of each island, and will help you find dive sites consistent with your level of experience. Chapter 2: Diving in St. Maarten, Chapter 3: Diving in Saba, and Chapter 4: Diving in St. Eustatius provide valuable information on currents, depth, and terrain specific to each site. Chapter 5: Marine Life of St. Maarten, Saba, and St. Eustatius describes the fishes, corals, and invertebrates specific to this area. Chapter 6: Safety provides information and tips to make your dives safe and enjoyable. Additionally, information about the local chamber operation and DAN is provided for your easy reference.

St. Maarten, Saba, and St. Eustatius are equally fascinating above water. Chapter 1: Overview of St. Maarten, Saba, and St. Eustatius contains information about hotels, dining, shopping, and travel. To help you plan your trip and save valuable time, Appendix 1 lists dive operators and Appendix 2 lists accommodations.

▲ *Encrusting corals and sponges cover the ship's anchor at the wreck of the H.M.S.* Proselyte, *St. Maarten. (Photo: J. Schnabel)*

◀ *Schooling squirrelfish (*Holocentrus rufus*) find shelter in narrow crevices at Double Wreck, St. Eustatius. (Photo: S. Swygert)*

The Rating System for Divers and Dive Sites

Divers are categorized as novice, intermediate, or advanced in an effort to help you select dives suitable to your individual levels of experience and capability.

We consider a *novice* diver to be someone in decent physical condition who has recently completed a scuba certification course, or a certified diver who has not been diving recently or has no experience in similar waters. We consider an *intermediate* diver to be a certified diver in excellent physical condition who has been diving actively for at least one year following certification and has been diving recently in similar waters. We consider an

Deepwater gorgonians (Iciligorgia schrammi) and encrusting red and orange sponges cover the rock ledges at Caroline's Reef, St. Eustatius. (Photo: J. Schnabel)

Ledges formed along the edges of large clumps of ballast stone provide shelter for the blackbar soldierfish. (Photo: J. Schnabel)

advanced diver to be someone who has completed an advanced scuba diving certification course, has been diving recently in similar waters, and is in excellent physical condition.

The dive sites are categorized as to **typical depth** which provides a range of depths the diver will most likely encounter during a dive at the site being discussed. The safe limit for sport diving has been set at 130 feet, and this guide does not recommend exceeding that limit.

Typical current conditions are listed as light, moderate, or heavy. Obviously, currents, waves, and weather can vary at times, and you need to assess your abilities responsibly. A good rule to follow is that if there is any apprehension at all about a certain dive, don't make it! Rather, move on to something you feel more comfortable with.

Expertise required is shown for each dive site—for novice, intermediate, and advanced levels of expertise as defined above. Access to the dive site is shown as either by shore or by boat, and the symbol * next to the name of the site denotes that the site is also good for snorkeling.

1

Overview of St. Maarten, Saba, and St. Eustatius

Christopher Columbus first sighted the Leeward Islands of St. Maarten, Saba, and St. Eustatius on St. Maarten Day, November 11, 1493, so it is thought that the island of St. Maarten was named in honor of this day. During the discovery years, most all of the Caribbean islands were inhabited primarily by Indians of the Arawak and Carib tribes. The Arawak Indians were peaceful by nature, greeting Columbus with gifts and friendly gestures. But the warlike Carib Indians rampaged throughout the islands, and Columbus avoided their areas.

It must have been an incredible sight to see St. Maarten as Columbus viewed it upon discovery—a beautifully green, mountainous island marked

Lush green mountains surround the turquoise waters of Great Bay, St. Maarten. (Photo: S. Swygert)

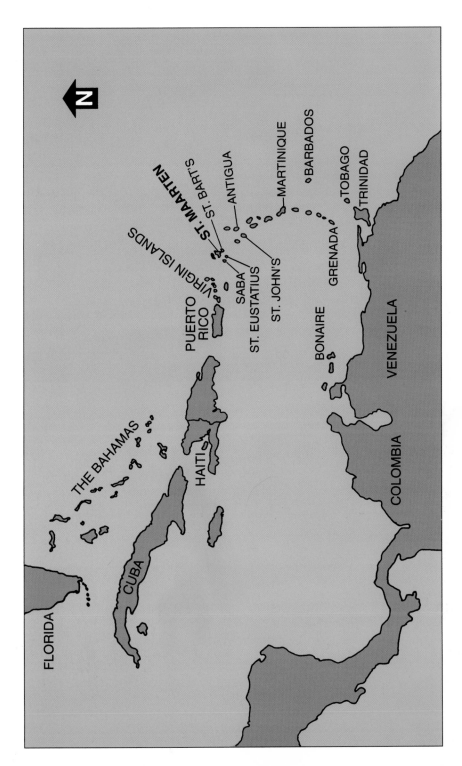

by Century Hill at an elevation of 1,200 feet, ringed by white sand beaches amid turquoise Caribbean waters. St. Maarten is surrounded by many other islands, all visible on a clear day. Within clear view, Saba lies just 26 miles to the south-southwest, St. Eustatius 30 miles to the south, Anguilla 11 miles to the north, and St. Bart's 11 miles to the southeast. The close proximity of the islands makes it easy to visit and dive them all in one vacation.

During the 1500s, the Spanish held the only settled colonies in the islands. As development began, the Indian populations were deported and enslaved in the copper mines of Hispaniola. Some Indians were eventually repatriated to their home islands, but today little is left of their culture. By 1636, the Dutch had begun pushing heavily into the Caribbean, chasing after the Spanish during the Eighty-Year War with Spain.

St. Maarten became important to the Dutch for its Great Salt Pond. Salt proved a valuable resource for the Dutch fishing fleets as a preservative for packing their fish. While the Dutch were busy colonizing the south of St. Maarten, the French were busy settling the northern portion of the island and growing sugar cane and tobacco. A unique agreement was finally made between the two countries in 1648 whereby the island was divided into

The summit of Mt. Scenery in Saba rises almost vertically to an elevation of 2,989 ft. above sea level. (Photo: J. Bourque)

These cannons of the restored Fort de Windt in St. Eustatius point seaward toward Buccaneer Bay and mark the site of once fierce battles. (Photo: J. Schnabel)

two parts. The French control the northern half of St. Maarten, known as Saint Martin, French West Indies, and the Dutch control the south, known as Sint Maarten, Netherlands, Antilles, thus forming two separate countries each with its own government, language, and customs. This phenomenon makes St. Maarten an interesting place to visit today.

Meanwhile, St. Eustatius, referred to as Statia by the local population, was becoming the center of trade in the Caribbean. Textiles, clothing, and furniture came from Europe, and rum, sugar, cotton, and tobacco were sent on the return voyages. Slaves from Africa were sent to the Americas and the Caribbean plantations, and salt was exported from St. Maarten. Saba, an almost vertical island about five miles long with Mt. Scenery rising to almost 3,000 feet above sea level, was almost impregnable to attack. The islands shifted in power between the British, Spanish, French, and Dutch during much of the 1600s and 1700s. However, by 1816, the Dutch controlled the islands of St. Maarten, Saba, St. Eustatius, Aruba, Bonaire, and Curacao—now referred to as the Islands of the Dutch Caribbean.

About 1.8 million tourists visit the Dutch Caribbean Islands annually. Most are Americans, Dutch, other Europeans, and South Americans. Tourism is quickly becoming the major industry of the islands. All the islands offer excellent snorkeling and scuba diving.

The Islands Today

St. Maarten. As St. Maarten is a beautiful, mountainous island surrounded by exquisite white sandy beaches, it has become a favorite with sun-seeking vacationers. Many invest in condominiums and time-share vacations. The waters off St. Maarten are clear and calm and are ideal for water sports activities. Sailing, windsurfing, waterskiing, snorkeling, scuba diving, jet skiing, and para-sailing are popular activities among visiting guests. Also, there are many good one-day sail and snorkel trips to neighboring islands, making it easy to enjoy the coral reefs and see tropical fishes.

Roads wind in and out along the French and Dutch coasts, rendering splendid panoramic views from convenient overlooks along the way. The Dutch capital city of Philipsburg runs along the beach at Great Bay and is called upon daily by an armada of cruise ships. Immaculate shops, outdoor cafes, and gourmet restaurants line narrow Front Street, which extends some 20 city blocks along the white sand beach edged with towering royal palm trees. As the island is shared by the French and Dutch, the dining possibilities here are unsurpassed at any other vacation destination in the Caribbean. Orient Bay on the French

The city of Philipsburg is the Dutch capital of St. Maarten and offers excellent attractions. (Photo: J. Schnabel)

▲ *Evening activities at the Great Bay Beach Hotel Casino. (Photo: J. Schnabel)*

◀ *Snorkelers, swimmers, and sunbathers enjoy the many fine beaches of St. Maarten, such as Maho Beach shown here. (Photo: J. Schnabel)*

side is considered a world-class windsurfing location, while Mullet Bay on the Dutch side offers championship golf overlooking Simpson Bay Lagoon. The rugged east coast is a series of secluded beaches and bays.

Diving activities are centered primarily out of Great Bay, Simpson Bay, Mullet Bay, and Marigot, with diving usually taking place along the southern coast of St. Maarten. Many dive excursions to nearby Saba and St. Eustatius are available daily. As air travel is planned to safe fly and dive altitudes, it is possible to have breakfast in St. Maarten, dive and have lunch in Saba or Statia, and return to St. Maarten for dinner.

Carnival in May is becoming a huge event, with colorful costumes, beautiful bodies, and cheering spectators. Parades continue for three days through the streets of Philipsburg, where spectators become almost intertwined with the parade and share a special time with friendly islanders.

Nightlife can encompass exciting discos, casinos, reggae music, dance shows, and a walk on the beach. Studio Seven at Maho Beach has a dance choreography show with a beach bikini theme. Frankie's at Great Bay imports talented bands from Caribbean islands featuring rock and reggae themes. The Calypso Bar at Simpson Bay hosts live calypso entertainment, and Cheri's Cafe has popular local bands with a variety of rock and reggae music. The small booklet *St. Maarten Nights* informs tourists about current nightlife activities, daytime events, shopping, and dining.

Saba. Rising almost vertically from the sea to 2,989 feet, the tiny island of Saba is breathtaking. Lush green mountain peaks are everywhere and the roads wind through the mountains, providing panoramic views of the towns and ocean below. Clusters of neatly painted white houses with red roofs color the verdant countryside around the villages and towns of Saba. The island is immaculately clean, a matter of immense pride among Sabans.

Captain C.R. Smith's memorial overlooking Saba provides a splendid view of the Caribbean Sea. (Photo: J. Schnabel)

This Catholic church at The Bottom is just one of many stone buildings to be seen in Saba. (Photo: J. Schnabel)

Saba director of tourism Glen Holm and photographer Susan Swygert study lava formations below Flat Point, Saba. (Photo: J. Schnabel)

The major industry is tourism. An average of 24,000 persons visit Saba annually, many via St. Maarten on day trips. Hiking and climbing are popular activities among visitors. The path up to the summit of Mt. Scenery (2,900 feet) is an incredible journey through seven altitudinal levels of change in vegetation. The peak rises up through the clouds to a beautiful rainforest in which the constant dripping of fresh water nourishes a multitude of tropical flowers, plants, and trees.

The tiny village of Windwardside (1,800 feet) has three small hotels and many guesthouses. Several small shops and one grocery store supply residents and tourists with a daily supply of food and sundries. There is a post office, a bank, restaurants, and a museum that displays priceless artifacts including some Indian relics. On the road below Windwardside is the capital town of The Bottom (669 feet), which has the island government offices and buildings, churches, and shops. Art galleries display watercolors and drawings by talented local artists. Fort Bay, just below The Bottom, is at sea level and is the island's only protected harbor. From here, dive boats depart to nearby coral reefs. The waters surrounding Saba are protected by a marine park. Concerned residents and protective legislation will no doubt keep Saba the "Unspoiled Queen" that she is as stated on the motor vehicle license plates. Serious seasoned travelers should not miss this magnificent island.

St. Eustatius (Statia). Statia moves at an unhurried pace. The people are friendly and relaxed, and a visit to this island seems to give one a feeling of stepping back in time. The island is rich in history and many of the old forts, historical sites, and buildings have been completely restored, creating an atmosphere similar to that of the 18th century. Mountainous extinct volcanoes at both ends of the island are connected by road over a relatively flat central terrain. The Quill at the southern end towers over the island at 1,960 feet. Inside the crater at the top of the Quill, there is a tropical rainforest with trails around the crater and down into the center. At the base of the crater lies a unique tree formed by two split trunks which join together high above ground; natives call it "The Marriage Tree." Scattered around the island are a few nice black sand beaches which provide tourists with a tranquil environment. Cozy, intimate guesthouses offer haven from the rest of the world as time seems to stand still.

Tourism, which has developed slowly over the last twenty years, is now Statia's largest industry, supporting many of the 1,800 islanders. Statia Terminals Oil Refinery and Depot, located in the north, is a major industrial development that employs some local people and seems not to impact the quality of daily life on Statia. The capital, Oranjestad, is divided into Upper Town on a hill above Gallows Bay and Lower Town which runs along the sea. The sunken remains of old Lower Town bear testimony to the pounding naval attack by British Admiral Rodney who punished Statia for being the first country to recognize the independence of the United States by saluting a visiting American ship with a volley of cannon fire. Statia never

Herbal medicine expert Mrs. Maisey relaxes at Park Place Gallery in Oranjestad, St. Eustatius. (Photo: J. Schnabel)

Photographer Jerry Schnabel is dwarfed by the huge "Marriage Tree," so named by local Statians. The tree is located in the rainforest of the Quill. (Photo: S. Swygert)

This restored study at the Historical Foundation Museum of Oranjestad, St. Eustatius, provides visitors a glimpse of earlier times during Admiral Rodney's rule. (Photo: J. Schnabel)

seemed to recover from the attack and the subsequent sacking of the island (perhaps until today when history is a part of everyone's life here). A museum in the rebuilt headquarters of Admiral Rodney displays artifacts from Statia's stormy past. Upper Town has small shops, a church, government offices, and restored Fort Orange complete with a stockade, cannons, and powder house. Lower Town has hotels and a series of black sand beaches popular among visiting tourists. Along the cobblestone streets of Lower Town, there is also a dive shop which runs trips to nearby coral reefs.

Hotels and Accommodations

St. Maarten, Saba, and St. Eustatius offer the visiting tourist three entirely different styles of accommodations. On St. Maarten, for instance, you would most likely stay in a fine hotel located on the beach with amenities such as room service, TV, telephones, casino, and a choice of restaurants. On Saba, the hotels and guesthouses are small and intimate, perched high on the mountain with an incredible view of the sea below, with friendly bars and quaint restaurants featuring fine cuisine. Statia has cozy, small hotels more functional in style, surrounded by a historical environment offering good food and reasonable prices. Refer to Appendix 2 for a listing of hotels and accommodations for the three islands.

St. Maarten. Perhaps the finest variety of accommodations in all the Caribbean islands can be found in St. Maarten. Luxury hotels, smart time-share villas, beautiful condominiums, sophisticated resorts, and comfortable guesthouses can be chosen in either a contemporary Dutch or charming French style. The Dutch side offers 22 hotels and 20 guesthouses while the French side has an additional 23 hotels and 8 guesthouses. Hotels such as the Maho Beach Resort, Royal Islander, Pelican Resort, Flamingo Beach

The ocean front terrace of the Great Bay Beach Hotel typifies the level of accommodations on St. Maarten.(Photo: J. Schnabel)

Lush greenery adorns the mountaintop at the Captain's Quarters hotel on Saba. (Photo: S. Swygert)

Resort, and Great Bay Beach Hotel will put you up in style on the southern coast closest to the dive sites. For a French touch, the La Samana, Radisson, Le Flamboyant, Royal Beach, and Grand Case Beach Club offer nice accommodations. Most major hotels have activities desks, which are well-equipped to properly advise you on water sports operators, tours of St. Maarten, and sightseeing trips to nearby islands.

Saba. Accommodations on Saba include pleasant 15-room hotels, colonial-style guesthouses, rental cottages, and private villas. Windwardside has the three hotels most popular with diving tourists—the Captain's Quarters, Scout's Place and Juliana's. At each of these small hotels you will find a restaurant, swimming pool, library, and gift shop. Windwardside, at an elevation of about 1,000 feet above sea level, has spectacular views both below and upward as Mt. Scenery towers over the village at an altitude of

The Old Gin House hotel on St. Eustatius is a completely restored group of seaside buildings. (Photo: J. Schnabel)

2,900 feet. Cranston's Inn, located at The Bottom, is a six-room inn rich in colonial atmosphere. The majority of cottages are in Windwardside; there are a few at Hell's Gate and one at St. John's. Reservations are recommended for all accommodations.

St. Eustatius. A variety of accommodations can be found in Statia, from historic hotels to apartments and guesthouses. The Old Gin House in Lower Town is a superbly restored colonial manor house with waterfront doubles, antique furnishings, a five-star restaurant, and a cozy, old-fashioned bar. Nearby, the Golden Era Hotel has waterfront rooms, pool, restaurant, and bar. Both are located within walking distance of Dive Statia. The Top of the Town Hotel, located near the airport, has modern doubles with TV, air-conditioning, and a good restaurant featuring native cuisine. Secluded in remote Zeelandia, La Maison Sur La Plage offers complete privacy with charming cottages overlooking a fine black sand beach. Various apartments and guesthouses in the Upper Town area provide tourists with many options in location and price.

Dining, Shopping, and Sightseeing

If you are into fine food and gourmet cuisine, there is no better place than St. Maarten in the Caribbean. Here, it's possible to dive and snorkel by day and enjoy world-class dining by night. Where to begin is difficult to say, as the tourist bureau points out that you could eat out every night for five months without repeating a choice. Philipsburg, Marigot, and Grand Case all have an ample variety of fine Italian, French, Indonesian, and Chinese restaurants. It is possible to have a classic evening at La Samana and spend over US$250 for dinner for two, while at the All You Can Eat Ribs in Philipsburg you could spend only US$25 on good food for two hungry divers. Good values are available due to healthy competition. Most restaurants are roadside and display their menus with prices for inspection. There are even Kentucky Fried Chicken, Pizza Hut, and other fast-food outlets available for budget-conscious vacationers.

As St. Maarten is a duty-free port, the prices on cameras, electronics equipment, jewelry, silver, and crystal rival those at any popular shopping destination. Boolchands has a large selection of cameras, lenses, and videos. The Shipwreck Shop has a good selection of books, postcards, and souvenirs. Penha has perfumes and clothing, and there are two Benetton clothing stores, one in Philipsburg, and one at Maho Beach. Little Switzerland and other fine jewelers offer solid gold watches, diamonds, and emeralds. Along

Shopping at downtown Philipsburg on the Dutch side and Marigot on the French side is a popular activity. (Photo: J. Schnabel)

the waterfront in Philipsburg, vendors display handcrafted items in an open market. Whether you come to St. Maarten to shop or not, it is certainly worth your time to investigate some of the bargains to be found here.

Touring the island will certainly include the Dutch capital city of Philipsburg. Here you will have a chance to meet some friendly islanders and see the sights along Front Street, such as the colorful old post office building. St. Maarten was once a city of forts. Wartime forts of the 17th and 18th century, where men fought fierce battles to defend the islands' rich trading centers, make for good sightseeing. Fort Amsterdam, Fort Willem, and two other forts overlook clear Caribbean waters. Fort Amsterdam was strategically positioned to overlook Great Bay and was the first Dutch fort in the Caribbean in 1631. Day trips to nearby islands are becoming more in demand with snorkel trips and lunch usually included. CAAP Aviation in Grand Case has packaged a set of aerial tours to Anguilla and St. Bart's. Snorkel sails to Prickly Pear Island near Anguilla leave daily from St. Maarten, as do catamaran trips to St. Bart's. Wilson McQueen offers high-speed boat trips to Saba for scuba diving, leaving in the morning and returning before nightfall.

Presently, there are 13 restaurants operating in Saba, and most hotels have their own restaurants offering a variety of seafood, steaks, and local dishes. The Brigadoon, Lollipop's and Cranston's all offer good local seafood and native cuisine. Guido's Italian Restaurant has good pizza, burgers, and sandwiches. Saba Chinese specializes in Cantonese food with an American menu also available.

The view from Fort Hill, St. Maarten, shows cruise ships where gunships sailed centuries ago. (Photo: J. Schnabel)

Local artist Heleen Cornet exhibits her work in her gallery in The Bottom, Saba. (Photo: J. Schnabel)

Around the Bend at Scout's Place has a wide variety of gifts, clothing, and souvenirs. Store hours vary and are usually posted at each shop. The Island Craft Shop, Saba Tropical Arts, and Peggy's Boutique all offer good selections of local arts and crafts as well as clothing and jewelry. "Saba spice" and "Saba lace" are both popular products from Saba. The spice is a fine liquor—rum, cinnamon, orange peel, sugar, and honey blended into a popular spirit of the Leeward Islands. Saba lace is an intricate embroidery done by local weavers and originally called Spanish work. The art of Saba lace embroidery was brought to the island as early as 1870. These handmade products are available at most of Saba's shops. Local artist Heleen Cornet lives in The Bottom and is a well-known contemporary painter. Her gallery, located at her home, displays a current collection of her work and is an interesting place to visit.

The tropical rainforest of Mt. Scenery on Saba can be visited by hiking up the trail which begins in Windwardside. (Photo: J. Schnabel)

The mountain road encircling Saba provides breathtaking vistas of the sea below, making an interesting drive filled with photo opportunities. Hiking and exploring are popular daytime activities on Saba. A hike up to the summit of Mt. Scenery is a little demanding but well worth the effort, as the view is spectacular. The peak is the rim of an extinct volcano which rises up to 2,955 feet above sea level. The vegetation along the trek to the top passes through several layers of changes from primary rainforest, treefern brake, palm brake, and elfin forest. Birds such as the bridled quail dove and purple-throated hummingbird can be sighted at elevation, while brown booby redtail hawks and sooty terns can be seen at lesser elevations. Overall, more than eighty species of birds live on or visit Saba.

In this restored dining room at the Old Gin House, fine cuisine is served amid a colonial atmosphere. (Photo: J. Schnabel)

Whether it's gourmet delights or native creole-style dishes, St. Eustatius offers many tempting dining possibilities. The Old Gin House in Lower Town serves five-star meals of seafood, steaks, and specialties set in a restored inn atmosphere. The Talk of the Town near the airport has good native dishes such as pork chops with peas and rice or grouper fingers. Cool Corner in Upper Town has burgers and native dishes priced for those on a budget. The King's Well in Lower Town features steaks, fish, wiener schnitzel, and pizza.

There are only a few shops on Statia located in Oranjestad's Upper Town. Park Place, owned by Barbara Lane, sells work of local artists in ceramics, straw products, and paintings. The Hole in the Wall Shop sells hand-

Giant trees, plants, flowers, and ferns flourish inside the crater of the Quill. Once an active volcano, it now shelters an isolated tropical rainforest. (Photo: J. Schnabel)

painted T-shirts, jewelry, and cotton dresses. Mazanga Gifts has a variety of gift items, books, postcards, magazines, snacks, and sodas. Dive Statia in Lower Town sells T-shirts, postcards, books, and diving equipment.

Statia is a great place for hiking and exploring. The Quill at the southern end of the island is an extinct volcano and a challenge to the experienced hiker. The rim of the crater is at an elevation of 1,960 feet, and there is a rough trail cut down into the crater where the rainforest can be explored. The iridescent hummingbird, found nowhere else in the world, seems to glow in the pale light of the Quill. Snorkeling over the remains of the sunken warehouses and taverns of Lower Town may turn up artifacts of the 1700s. Blue slave beads once used as trading currency by the merchants and slaves, clay pipes, and shards of pottery are the only artifacts allowed to be removed from Statia. The museum at Upper Town is an amazing collection of historical artifacts, well preserved and appropriately displayed. Here you can trace, with the help of charts, the historical events which preceded modern-day Statia.

These blue slave beads were once used by merchants as trading currency in St. Eustatius. (Photo: J. Schnabel)

Transportation

Travel to St. Maarten is quite easy, as many airlines offer direct flights from major U.S. cities. Travel to Saba and St. Eustatius is by way of St. Maarten. Inter-island flights by Windward Airlines to Saba and Statia leave St. Maarten several times daily, making travel to the out islands very convenient. American Airlines has both direct flights to St. Maarten and flights through its hub in Puerto Rico from Boston, Dallas, Los Angeles, Miami, New York, and Raleigh-Durham. KLM has flights from Amsterdam, London, Paris, Rome, and other European cities. ALM has flights to St. Maarten via Curacao from Miami. Pan American has daily flights from Miami and New York. Continental flies daily from Newark, New Jersey. Other airlines, including Air France, have daily flights to St. Maarten, making it an accessible destination from the U.S. and Europe. Other means of travel to St. Maarten include major cruise ship lines. Contact your travel agent now to plan your trip.

Customs and Immigration

The islands of St. Maarten, Saba, and Statia are part of the Netherlands Antilles and are a Dutch protectorate. Entry requires proof of citizenship such as a passport and a return ticket. Customs and immigration cards are passed out by most airlines prior to disembarkation and must be completed upon entry to the country. As St. Maarten is a duty-free port, you can take advantage of the new U.S. and Canadian travel allowances. U.S. citizens may now bring home $600 worth of articles acquired abroad. Additional foreign purchases up to US$1,000 are assessed at a flat 10%. Foreign works of art, such as drawings, paintings, sculptures, and certain artistic jewelry, are duty-free. Returning Canadians may bring in up to C$300 worth of purchases if away for seven days or more, otherwise, C$100 is exempt. The next C$300 is taxed at a reduced rate of 20%.

Departure tax from the islands is US$10, and airline reconfirmation 24 hours prior to departure is advisable.

Foreign Exchange

The currency used on St. Maarten, Saba, and Statia is the Netherlands Antilles florin (NA Fls.). The florin or guilder is a sound currency which is backed by gold on the foreign exchange. The U.S. dollar is widely used here also and it buys 1.77 NA Fls. at the official rate of purchase. Rates will vary between 1.75 to 1.80 for travelers checks and foreign checks. Most service establishments deal in U.S. dollars, however, it is advisable to convert a small amount of dollars to guilders for odd purchases.

2

Diving in St. Maarten

Because of the fine hotels, good diving, and exciting nightlife, St. Maarten is an ideal location to enjoy diving mixed with fun land-based activities. Scuba diving, snorkeling, jet skiing, para-sailing, and waterskiing are popular. Snorkel trips can be booked through independent operators and most hotels. As St. Maarten is surrounded by undeveloped smaller islands, day sailing trips to the outlying islands for snorkeling are popular and recommended.

Banded butterflyfish (Chaetodon striatus)*, usually seen swimming in pairs, roam the reefs of St. Maarten. (Photo: J. Schnabel)*

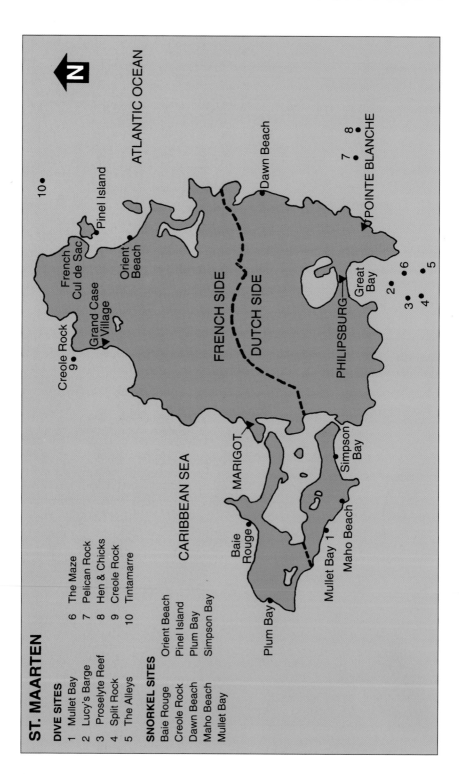

ST. MAARTEN

DIVE SITES

1 Mullet Bay
2 Lucy's Barge
3 Proselyte Reef
4 Split Rock
5 The Alleys

6 The Maze
7 Pelican Rock
8 Hen & Chicks
9 Creole Rock
10 Tintamarre

SNORKEL SITES

Baie Rouge
Creole Rock
Dawn Beach
Maho Beach
Mullet Bay

Orient Beach
Pinel Island
Plum Bay
Simpson Bay

N

ATLANTIC OCEAN

CARIBBEAN SEA

FRENCH SIDE

DUTCH SIDE

Pinel Island

French
Cul de Sac

Orient
Beach

Grand Case
Village

Creole Rock
9

10

Dawn Beach

PHILIPSBURG

Great
Bay

POINTE BLANCHE

7
8

2
6
3
4
5

MARIGOT

Baie
Rouge

Simpson
Bay

Maho Beach

Mullet Bay 1

Plum Bay

Corals, sponges, gorgonians, and the common sea fan (Gorgonia ventalina) form coral reefs atop boulders and wrecks off St. Maarten's southeastern coast. (Photo: S. Swygert)

As St. Maarten is surrounded by undeveloped smaller islands, day sailing trips to the outlying islands for snorkeling are popular and recommended.

The leeward southern coastline of St. Maarten is almost always accessible by dive boats, and it is here that most diving takes place. Numerous sites are found along the east coast, from Tintamarre Island at the north to Hen & Chicks Rocks at the south. However, due to prevailing winds, the sites

Snorkeling

Snorkeling and swimming attract thousands annually to the inviting waters of St. Maarten. For this reason, we shall include some useful information about recommended snorkeling sites. As weather conditions change from time to time, it is recommended that snorkelers contact local dive shops for tips on where snorkeling is best for their level of expertise.

Dawn Beach is a popular snorkeling site on the east coast of St. Maarten. (Photo: S. Swygert)

wrecks, and rock formations at varying depths. Wall diving is not offered on St. Maarten and perhaps accounts for the lack of hard-core divers coming here. But diving on St. Maarten suits beginners and experienced divers alike who prefer to dive and enjoy afterwards all that St. Maarten has to offer.

Dive facilities are expanding and new operators are bringing in larger dive boats capable of reaching outlying locations. Experienced pros such as Leroy French of Ocean Explorers Dive Center and Tom and Adrienne of Tradewinds Dive Center can offer valuable insight and advice about diving on St. Maarten. There are also live-aboard boats that make St. Maarten their jumping-off point. The eastern sites, while weather-dependent, offer good diving on small rock islands. Here the dives focus on the boulders of coral and variety of marine life surrounding each island or rock. For a detailed listing of dive operators, refer to Appendix 1.

Snorkeling Sites

Dawn Beach lies about midway along the eastern coastline of St. Maarten on the Dutch side. It is a fabulous beach with good reefs for snorkeling. A

Day trips to Pinel Island on the French side of St. Maarten are popular with snorkelers. Regular ferry service is available from French Cul de Sac. (Photo: J. Schnabel)

breaking reef runs close to shore and provides many good snorkeling sites. Do not dive here when the water is rough or the weather stormy.

Creole Rock is located next to Bell Point outside of Grand Case in the Baie de Grand Case on the French side. As its name implies, this site is a large offshore rock formation accessible only by boat. Shallow corals and other marine life abound here. Silversides (small silvery fish) glitter in the shafts of light from a small cave in the rock. Check with local dive operators for trip schedules to this popular site.

Mullet Bay, oceanside at the Mullet Beach Resort, is often used as a training dive location. Snorkeling is done here close to shore and along the beach and rocks on the south side. A low-lying reef closely parallels the shoreline.

Maho Beach is a large white sand beach located on the west end of the Juliana Airport stretching north to south along Maho Bay. There is a small reef area around the rock formations on the south side of the beach. Numerous tropical fish can be seen here.

Baie Rouge on the French side is a fantastic beach with good snorkeling. The east side has some rock and cave formations which provide shelter for various tropicals.

Pinel Island is accessible by a local ferry service departing from French Cul de Sac. The reefs here are ideal for snorkeling, and the beach is well-kept. One could stay a full day on the island exploring, snorkeling, and beach-combing.

Orient Beach is located along the northeastern coastline of the French side. There are concession stands at the beach entrance area where most people can be seen snorkeling. Close to shore, there is a predominant sand bottom, and reefs are apparent further offshore.

Plum Bay lies along the westernmost tip of St. Maarten on the French side. Here, a long beach provides good snorkeling on reefs close to shore.

Simpson Bay has a good snorkeling reef just in front of Ocean Explorers Dive Center, owned by veteran St. Maarten diver Leroy French. You can learn about local fishes from the shop's staff, and purchase ID cards and books describing the various marine life found in St. Maarten waters.

Check your road map for directions to these popular beaches. Day trips to St. Bart's, Anguilla, and Prickly Pear Island are also available for snorkelers.

The Dive Sites

We will discuss ten of the most popular dive sites on St. Maarten. Many attempts have been made to install moorings on St. Maarten, but due to heavy weather at times, the moorings usually don't hold fast. Hence, dive operators anchor carefully in sandy areas at known dive sites.

The average visibility will be about 60 to 100 feet. The dive sites are at fixed depths on flat, sandy bottoms with boulders and large patch reef configurations. Average diving depths usually range from 30 to 70 feet, currents are light to moderate, and the surge can be strong in bad weather. Each dive site has a variety of gorgonians, sea fans, hard corals, and a cross section of Caribbean fishes. There are also wrecks that attract colorful schools of fish.

All diving excursions are made by dive boats. At Mullet Bay, Maho Divers conducts beach training dives and night dives from its white sandy beach area. This is a peaceful and controlled location for a beginning diving experience. Night dives here are colorful, with flame scallops protruding from undercut ledges. The symbol * next to the site name indicates that the site is also good for snorkeling.

Mullet Bay * 1

Typical Depth Range:	12–25 feet
Typical Current Conditions:	Light
Expertise Required:	Novice
Access:	Shore

This is a shallow sand beach dive site with some flat outcroppings of coral. It is excellent for snorkeling, as fish are seen along the ironshore portions of the bay. Also, this is a popular training area for beginning divers due to ease of entry and calm conditions. Night diving can also be done here, and various invertebrates can be found among the flat ledges of coral and rock.

The tranquil waters at Mullet Bay Beach provide good conditions for snorkeling. (Photo: S. Swygert)

Lucy's Barge 2

Typical Depth Range:	40–55 feet
Typical Current Conditions:	Light to Moderate
Expertise Required:	Intermediate
Access:	Boat

Located about one mile south of Fort Amsterdam Rock, the barge, officially named *HVALD,* is named after owner Lucy Baker who donated it as a dive site. Lucy's Barge is 100 feet long by 27 feet wide and rests in 55 feet of water. The barge was sunk on January 23, 1991, by divers from Tradewinds Dive Center, Bobbie's Marina, and Divesport of St. Maarten. Today, the barge is in an area of rocky terrain with scattered gorgonians and sea fans. Barracudas, jacks, and Spanish mackerel can be seen here. Rock beauties, parrotfish, French angelfish, and soldierfish are common to the area. Occasionally, crevalle jacks swim through this area in search of tiny bait-fish schools—their source of food.

The wreck Lucy's Barge is a recent addition to the dive sites of St. Maarten. (Photo: J. Schnabel)

Proselyte Reef * 3

Typical Depth Range:	15–45 feet
Typical Current Conditions:	Moderate
Expertise Required:	Intermediate
Access:	Boat

Located about 1.2 miles south of Fort Amsterdam Rock, the wreck of the H.M.S. *Proselyte* is the most popular dive site on St. Maarten. The *Proselyte* is a 133-foot-long British war frigate carrying 32 guns; some of the cannons are still visible and encrusted with coral. The ship was given to the

Proselyte *Reef is by far the most popular St. Maarten dive site. This resident trumpetfish* (Aulostomus maculatus) *travels the reef and shelters in the soft corals. (Photo: J. Schnabel)*

The immense anchor at Proselyte *Reef makes an excellent photo opportunity. (Photo: J. Schnabel)*

British by a mutinous Dutch crew on June 8, 1786, at Greenrock, Scotland. The *Proselyte* crashed into Man O' War Shoals in Great Bay, St. Maarten, on September 2, 1801. The crew of 215 survived.

The wreck is visible from the surface and is completely encrusted with coral. Anchors and cannons are scattered and encrusted in the wreckage. Gorgonians and sea fans cover the reef area. The *Proselyte* Reef rises from 45 feet vertically to within 15 feet of the surface.

Several large rock outcroppings surround the wreck area. The wreck and rocks are thick with red and yellow sponge growth; purple candle sponges grow upwards from the wreck. Marine life includes a resident yellow trumpetfish, soldierfish, horse-eye jacks, barracuda, and French angelfish. When the water is calm, this is an ideal snorkeling location, but not advised when the wind is blowing.

Split Rock (Cuda Alley)   4

Typical Depth Range:	20–55 feet
Typical Current Conditions:	Moderate
Expertise Required:	Intermediate
Access:	Boat

This dive site is just south of the *Proselyte* Reef. A large rock formation rises vertically, reaching to within 20 feet of the surface. The rock formation is heavily encrusted with sponges, gorgonians, and sea fans. Large ledges and rocks lie to the east and south of the main reef area. The split rock takes its name from the east-west groove in the coral. Soldierfish seek safety in the ledges and cuts in the coral rock, often dwelling in undercut ledges. There are colorful queen triggerfish, French angelfish, octopus, and barracuda. The sea floor is an area of sand with rock outcroppings; the outlying rocks make up small coral communities with resident damselfish. The area is a good macrophotography area abundant with arrow crabs, bristle worms, and banded coral shrimp. Horse-eye jacks and Spanish mackerel also swim through this area.

*The dive site of Split Rock is often referred to as Cuda Alley because of its several resident barracudas (*Sphyraena barracuda*). (Photo: S. Swygert)*

Typical Depth Range:	20–65 feet
Typical Current Conditions:	Moderate
Expertise Required:	Intermediate
Access:	Boat

Located to the southeast of split rock in 65 feet of water, the Alleys consist of a series of large rock formations. Running south at the base of the rocks are caves and ledges. The rocks are encrusted with orange and yellow sponges; purple candle sponges also grow here. Gorgonians and sea fans

These blackbar soldierfish (Myripristis jacobus) seek shelter in the numerous ledges of the Alleys. (Photo: S. Swygert)

This large tugboat cable has become a permanent part of the reef known as Cable Reef. (Photo: J. Hilgers)

grow up from the rocks and sea floor, and the large rock formations create alleyways between them, perhaps attributing to the name of the site. The sandy areas often shelter southern rays. Rock beauties, French angelfish, and soldierfish are easily observed swimming throughout the coral alleys. Schools of barracuda are common, and photo opportunities abound here. Keep a close eye on the boat's anchor because it is easy to become confused as to your location—all of the formations seem to be a lot alike. Just to the south of the Alleys, there is a long tugboat cable draped over the reef; this site is known as Cable Reef, which is usually dived as a separate site depending on where the boat anchors.

The Maze 6

Typical Depth Range:	20–45 feet
Typical Current Conditions:	Moderate to Strong
Expertise Required:	Intermediate
Access:	Boat

The Maze lies just one-fourth mile east of *Proselyte* Reef and two miles south of Great Bay Harbor. Some elkhorn coral grows on top of the reef in 25 feet of water. Small caves are etched out of the sides of the reef and provide homes for nurse sharks. Turtles can occasionally be seen here, along with rays, French angelfish, and barracudas. Tunnels, which divers can easily swim through, create a maze-like pattern in the large coral rock formations. Here, you will want to keep track of where you are, as it is easy to become confused; your dive guide will be happy to show you through the maze. Large schools of Bermuda chub swim through this area, and bigeyes and soldierfish are plentiful. Isolated stands of pillar coral are growing on top of some of the rock formations.

A series of caves and tunnels form a natural maze from which this dive site takes its name, the Maze. (Photo: J. Schnabel)

Typical Depth Range:	20–55 feet
Typical Current Conditions:	Moderate
Expertise Required:	Advanced
Access:	Boat

Pelican Rock is a large rock protrusion to the west of Hen & Chicks. A sand bottom surrounds the rock, and there are large boulders broken off from the main rock underwater surrounding Pelican Rock. The boulders create natural shelters for trumpetfish, soldierfish, lobsters, and crabs. Invertebrates seek the protection of small grooves throughout the boulders of coral. A myriad of fish inhabit the territory, making this an interesting dive when weather permits.

Pelican Rock on the Atlantic east side of St. Maarten lies offshore from Pointe Blanche and can only be dived in good weather. (Photo: J. Schnabel) ▶

Submerged boulders surrounding Pelican Rock form a naturally colorful coral reef. (Photo: J. Schnabel) ▼

Hen & Chicks 8

Typical Depth Range:	20–70 feet
Typical Current Conditions:	Moderate to Strong
Expertise Required:	Advanced
Access:	Boat

Located two miles off Pointe Blanche, this site is marked by one large rock and two smaller ones to the south—hence the name Hen & Chicks. This site differs from the others in that it is a mini wall which drops from the surface to 70 feet deep. The upper edge of the reef begins with elkhorn corals and encrusting yellow and orange sponges. Here, you can see numerous tropical species, with moray eels, pufferfish, and rays in the sand bottom at 70 feet.

The view from Pointe Blanche shows Pelican Rock to the left side with Hen & Chicks Rocks visible to the right in the background. (Photo: S. Swygert)

Creole Rock * 9

Typical Depth Range:	10–25 feet
Typical Current Conditions:	Moderate
Expertise Required:	Novice
Access:	Boat

The rock formation known as Creole Rock is just outside the town of Grand Case on the north side of St. Maarten. Here, a large rock island protrudes upward from only 25 feet of water. Usually, this is a calm, protected area, ideal for beginning snorkelers and divers. For this reason, it has become a popular site, and daily snorkel trips are conducted to Creole Rock from many dive operations on the French side. Soft corals include gorgonians and sea fans, while hard corals include brain corals, star corals, elkhorn corals, and boulder corals. Tropicals such as rock beauties, butterflyfish, and parrotfish adorn the coral formations. At one point, there is an overhang formation where schools of silversides often school up, creating a great photo opportunity.

Creole Rock shown here is a popular dive site located just offshore from Grand Case on the French side. (Photo: S. Swygert)

Tintamarre (Tugboat Wreck) 10

Typical Depth Range:	40 feet
Typical Current Conditions:	Moderate
Expertise Required:	Intermediate
Access:	Boat

About one mile from Pinel Island lies the small uninhabited island of Tintamarre. A tugboat has been sunk here to form an interesting dive site. The tug is about 40 feet long and is becoming covered with coral growth. Tropical fish such as groupers, butterflyfish, rock beauties, and soldierfish are common. Half-day trips to the wreck are offered by dive shops on the French side of St. Maarten, and the site is becoming popular with visiting divers. The wreck sits upright in about 40 feet of water and is a good subject for underwater photography and video.

Tintamarre Island is accessible only by boat and is becoming a popular diving spot. (Photo: J. Schnabel)

3

Diving in Saba

Due to its natural attractions both above and below the water, Saba is fast becoming known as one of the better dive destinations in the Caribbean. Because accommodations are at an elevation of about 1,010 feet above sea level, you will have to drive down to Fort Bay, the only marina on Saba, to board the dive boats. This is only about a ten-minute drive and has a splendid view of the valleys below. Saba Deep, run by Mike Meyers and Maureen Behudin, has its dive shop, boutique, and restaurant located here at Fort Bay. They have two twin-engine, 27-foot dive boats, a charming bar and restaurant, and an efficient dive shop all located in the same building for divers' convenience. This is a good gathering place and a popular haven for divers to share stories over some hearty food. Sea Saba, owned by Lou and Joan Bourque and John and Lynn Magor, has two diesel-powered dive boats, one a 36-footer and the other a 40-footer. Both boats have ample room for cameras and handle the seas well. Both Joan and John are accomplished photographers and will gladly assist visiting divers with their photo

The rich colors and varied marine life of Saba are attracting divers and underwater photographers in increasing numbers. The Twilight Zone is shown here. (Photo: J. Schnabel)

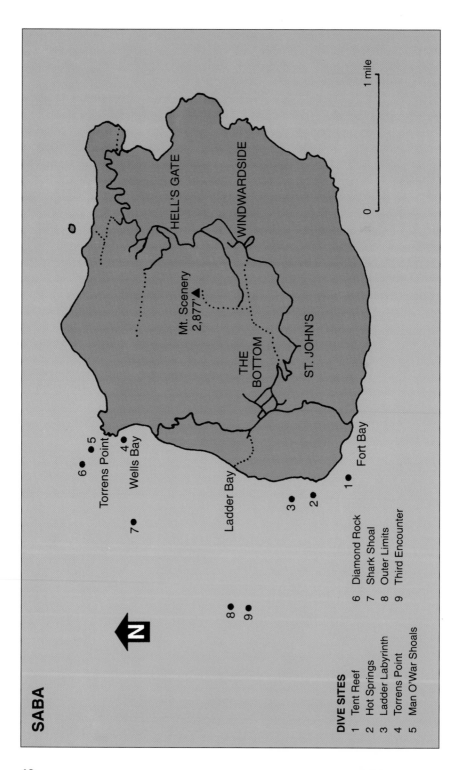

SABA

N

DIVE SITES

1 Tent Reef
2 Hot Springs
3 Ladder Labyrinth
4 Torrens Point
5 Man O'War Shoals

6 Diamond Rock
7 Shark Shoal
8 Outer Limits
9 Third Encounter

HELL'S GATE

WINDWARDSIDE

Mt. Scenery
2,877'

THE
BOTTOM

ST. JOHN'S

Torrens Point

Wells Bay

Ladder Bay

Fort Bay

0   1 mile

requirements. Sea Saba is located at Windwardside and has a large retail dive shop where divers can purchase needed items as well as view paintings of dive sites by Joan Bourque. A visit here will be filled with talk about recent dive experiences. Located in Fort Bay is Wilson's Dive Shop owned by Wilson McQueen who brings divers over to Saba from St. Maarten on his mother vessel, *Styles*. Mr. McQueen's fast, Zodiac-type dive boats handle the visiting divers on Saba.

Almost all diving in Saba is done from boats except for the snorkel trail at Torrens Point in Wells Bay. Boat trips to the dive sites are short 10-minute rides, and then you're in the water. So even if the sea is a little rough, it won't matter because you will be underwater and home soon. Usually the dive boats run trips three times per day, and boat night dives are available. The diving encompasses all levels of expertise due to the varied nature of the undersea topography. Both beginners and experienced divers will enjoy Saba's offerings.

During a typical dive, you will see colorful sponges, schools of fish, splendid hard corals, gorgonians, and sea fans. Turtles, stingrays, nurse sharks, and reef blacktip sharks are frequently seen as well, rounding out the array of marine life. The underwater terrain includes vertical formations known as pinnacles or seamounts, large boulders and rocks encrusted with corals and sponges, and spur and groove coral formations. The offshore pinnacles are the tops of undersea mountains rising up from the sea floor thousands of feet below. The fact that the pinnacles reach up to within diving depths

*The queen angelfish (*Holacanthus ciliaris*) a common sight on the reefs of Saba, is thought to be the most beautiful of all Caribbean fishes. (Photo: S. Swygert)*

The Saba Marine Park

The Saba Marine Park was established in 1987 with the objective to preserve and manage an enormous resource of the Saba marine environment. This project was founded by the World Wildlife Fund—Netherlands, the Prince Bernhard Fund, and the Dutch and Saban Governments.

The park area encircles the entire island of Saba and is divided into four major zones: anchorage zone, multi-use zone (fishing and diving), recreational diving zone (no fishing, no anchoring), and all-purpose recreational zone (swimming, boating, diving, and fishing). The park waters encompass an area from the high water line down to a depth of 200 feet, as well as two offshore mounts.

Administration of the park is handled by the Saba Conservation Foundation. The island government subsidizes the foundation for park staff salaries. Currently, the park is close to becoming self-sustaining through the collection of user fees (presently, visiting divers pay one dollar per dive in the park), souvenir sales, and private donations.

Reef Conservation

The Saba Marine Park maintains a working mooring buoy system; all dive boats must use the moorings. This prevents damage to precious corals caused by dragging anchors toppling delicate coral heads. The marine park has an office at Fort Bay managed by Susan Walker White. There, information is available on the preservation of the marine environment. Furthermore, presentations and lectures are offered free of charge to all dive groups visiting the island. The park manager is assisted by park rangers who maintain and oversee the use of the reef mooring buoys. The marine park also oversees and manages a multi-place hyperbaric recompression chamber facility operated by a staff of specially trained volunteers. This recompression chamber serves nearby islands, including St. Maarten and St. Eustatius.

has made Saba a unique destination among savvy divers. Currents are usually light, but occasional storms create strong surge and currents.

Generally, the weather is sunny and the seas calm. Because Saba is so impressive above water, it is an ideal place for a diving vacation. For a detailed listing of dive operators, refer to Appendix 1.

The numbered white face-mask plaque shown here in the foreground marks the snorkel trail at Torrens Point. (Photo: J. Schnabel)

The Dive Sites

There are presently 26 moored dive sites around Saba. We shall discuss nine of the most popular sites that represent a cross section of the diving around Saba.

The offshore pinnacles usually begin in depths of 80 to 100 feet, plummeting vertically to depths of 1,000 feet. They are characterized by hills and

---

Saba Marine Park Regulations

While diving in the Saba Marine Park (S.M.P.), please adhere to the following park regulations:

1. Spearfishing and conch and turtle collecting are prohibited except for Saba residents while free diving. Restrictions are placed on the size, amounts, and seasons in which each are collected. All catches must be reported to the S.M.P. manager. For more information, see the S.M.P. manager.
2. The use of poisons, chemicals, or explosives is prohibited.
3. Do not take any coral or other bottom-dwelling marine animals or plants.
4. Divers can avoid damage to coral and sponges by proper buoyancy control. Do not sit or stand on corals—they are living animals.
5. Do not anchor in coral; anchor only in sandy areas outside the diving zones. Anchoring is permitted only in anchorage zones.
6. Boats from 50 to 100 feet long are restricted to the orange mooring buoys. White buoys are intended for boats up to 50 feet long. A few yacht moorings—marked with yellow buoys—are available in the Ladder Bay and Wells Bay anchorage zones. A brochure is available entitled Anchorages and Mooring Buoys.
7. The use of a dive mooring is limited to the time necessary for one dive (up to two hours).
8. Fishing is not allowed in the recreational diving zone (refer to the *Park Service Zoning* map).
9. Do not litter.
10. Passage within the S.M.P. by vessels or boats must always stay 150 meters seaward of any boat flying a dive flag (except in an emergency and when the dive boat has been contacted). This rule also applies to dinghies.

valleys of corals and sponges, deepwater gorgonians, purple tube sponges, iridescent vase sponges, and mountainous star corals. Sharks circle the pinnacles; moray eels, coral crabs, frogfish, and pelagics all are common sights.

Other mountain peaks, like Man O' War Shoals, rise from 70 to 80 feet of sand and have much of the color and interest of the deep pinnacles but afford more bottom time for exploration. Tent Reef, on the other hand, is a long ledge formation dropping from 10 feet deep on top to as much as 40 feet below. The vertical ledge of coral at Tent Reef makes for interesting exploration, and night dives are easily conducted here.

Close to shore, broken-off large rock boulders have piled up over the decades to form a labyrinth of tunnels and passages through the coral. A dive here usually follows a dive to one of the deeper pinnacles. Other spur and groove reef formations lie just outside the rock and boulder area. Coral ridges or spurs and sand valleys or grooves extend outward from as shallow as 20 feet to as deep as 60 feet or more, where they break up into sandy slopes. You can even detect the warmth from the underlying volcano by just putting your fingers into the sand in some areas. As the coral reefs and geological formations of Saba are quite unique, a marine park has been created to preserve their beauty. The symbol * next to the site name indicates that the site is also good for snorkeling.

Tent Reef * 1

Typical Depth Range:	10–40 feet
Typical Current Conditions:	Light
Expertise Required:	Novice
Access:	Boat

Tent Reef lies just west of Fort Bay opposite Tent Bay. This is probably the most popular shallow reef dive on Saba. It is made up of a large rock ledge paralleling the shoreline, 10 to 15 feet on top and dropping to 40 feet deep in some places. On the north end of the ledge, the depth falls off to

Saba Marine Park manager Susan Walker White inspects the delicate corals of Tent Reef. (Photo: J. Schnabel)

Natural caves and tunnels are formed at Tent Reef by massive boulders and wall formations. (Photo: J. Schnabel)

deeper water, and this area is another dive site known as Tent Reef Deep. The rock ledge is undercut and forms small caves and tunnels in some places. The rock faces are encrusted with corals, sponges, sea fans, and gorgonians. Schools of blackbar soldierfish seek shelter in the caves, playful coneys occupy coral grooves, and turtles pass through frequently.

Adding color to the reef are orange, yellow, red, and pink sponges that filter-feed nutrients from the water column, pumping gallons of water through their openings daily. Orange cup corals (tubastrea coral) grow on the ledges and undercuts. The recommended dive plan for this area is to proceed into the current from the mooring along the ledge, and return to your dive boat using the ledge as a guide. During the course of the dive, it is interesting to explore the fallen boulders near the ledge. This is an excellent site for photography; macro possibilities are endless, and night diving here will produce vivid, color-filled images of the many corals and invertebrates.

Typical Depth Range:	15–45 feet
Typical Current Conditions:	Light
Expertise Required:	Novice
Access:	Boat

Located about halfway between Ladder Bay and Tent Bay ranging close to shore and extending out about 200 meters, Hot Springs is named after the characteristic hot water vents in the shallow zone. Warm water can be felt coming out of the sand vents; the water is heated by underground lava concentrations.

The shallow region here is made up of encrusting boulders which have been formed from volcanic eruptions. Over the years, corals have grown over the boulders and sponges have encrusted them, creating a reef system throughout this area. The tops of the boulders are covered in fire corals and elkhorn corals, and gorgonians and sea fans decorate the reef. Isolated pillar coral stands, and one in particular near the mooring, reach heights of four feet. Coneys and graysbies are plentiful among the corals; always curious, they appear to greet visiting divers. Scrawled filefish and Bermuda chubs swim regularly through the shallows.

Extending out from the shallow zone, the reef slopes to 45 feet of sand which is interrupted by large barrel sponges and low-lying patch reefs. Put your hands into the sand and you will probably feel the warmth from the molten lava deep below the surface.

Cleaning stations are evident throughout mountainous star coral and brain coral areas. Juvenile Spanish hogfish, neon gobies, and yellow wrasses make up most of the cleaning fishes active here.

Warm-water vents can be felt in the sand near yellow sulfur deposits here at Hot Springs. (Photo: J. Schnabel)

Typical Depth Range:	15–45 feet
Typical Current Conditions:	Light
Expertise Required:	Novice
Access:	Boat

   This site is located on the south side of Ladder Bay less than one-half mile from shore. It is characterized by a spur and groove coral system with coral spurs extending from shore to the west with sand valleys in between. The sand is typically the gray-black type associated with volcanic formations. Yellow

Large growths of pillar coral (Dendrogyra cylindrus) *identify the undersea terrain at Ladder Labyrinth. (Photo: J. Schnabel)*

areas in the sand are warm to the touch, indicating sulfur from activity below ground. The shallows are typically composed of large coral-encrusted boulders with elkhorn coral atop some of them. Sea fans and gorgonians grow to enormous proportions in this region. Spotted moray eels can be seen poking their heads out of cracks in the coral. Depths of 45 feet have sand valleys between undercut ledges and caves, providing shelter for an occasional nurse shark. As usual, coneys and graysbies are everywhere; blue tangs, butterflyfish, and white spotted filefish are common in this region.

Large barrel sponges can be seen near the mooring, as can an occasional iridescent vase sponge. Swimming through the spurs and grooves can easily disorient the diver, so pay close attention to your depth and direction. A compass is recommended as a directional aid for returning to the large anchor mooring.

*Curious coneys (*Epinephelus fulvus*) make friends with visiting divers. (Photo: J. Schnabel)*

Torrens Point * 4

Typical Depth Range:	10–40 feet
Typical Current Conditions:	Light
Expertise Required:	Novice
Access:	Shore or boat

This site at Wells Bay is significant because it is the location of the snorkeling trail. An underwater snorkel trail is marked by numbered face-mask plaques which correspond to a snorkel chart of the area. The trail takes the snorkeler through a maze of coral and rock formations. The north end of the bay has a large cave; sandy valleys between the rock boulders in the bay shelter stingrays, nurse sharks, and eels. Turtles are common here also. The mooring lies in the center of the bay. The dive plan usually is to proceed north to the cave and return by way of the large boulder coral formations which arc down and out to the south.

Macro life includes numerous flamingo tongue shells, fingerprint cowries, and sponge decorator crabs. The elkhorn coral formations among the upper edges of the rocks are exquisite. Sea fans and gorgonians sway with the current, preyed upon by an army of flamingo tongue shells. Parrotfish, squirrelfish, soldierfish, and hatchetfish swim in the undercut caves. The caves also provide shelter to banded coral shrimp, flame scallops, and other invertebrates.

Large elkhorn corals (Acropora palmata) grow close to the surface, making Torrens Point an excellent location for shallow diving or snorkeling. (Photo: J. Schnabel)

53

Typical Depth Range:	10–70 feet
Typical Current Conditions:	Moderate
Expertise Required:	Intermediate
Access:	Boat

Protruding up to as shallow as 10 to 15 feet from a depth of 70 feet of sand, this is one of the best locations in the Caribbean for wide-angle photography. At the base of the large vertical rock formation lies a sandy, flat bottom in 70 feet of water, which affords the diver ample time for explo-

Soft coral polyps of the deepwater gorgonian (Iciligorgia schrammi) *extend out to filter-feed nutrients from the water column. (Photo: S. Swygert)*

Colorful crevices, seemingly etched in the undersea mountains of Man O' War Shoals, provide excellent underwater photo opportunities. (Photo: J. Schnabel)

ration. The mooring is located just south of the site, and your guide will lead you over to the split rock formation.

The dive plan here is to swim around the circular formation, slowly working your way up the wall face and back to your starting point. This plan increases safety and enables you to see the different levels of activity here. Be sure and leave at least 800 lbs. of air for the swim back to the boat.

At the base of the rock are enormous barrel sponges and deepwater gorgonians; the rock splits in the center, forming two major pinnacles. The natural ravine between the pinnacles is a colorful scene of deepwater gorgonians, barrel sponges, and thriving schools of fish.

Throughout the formation are yellow and purple tube sponges; encrusting red, orange, and yellow sponges color the reef profusely. Coneys, rock beauties, graysbies, and blue tangs dominate the scene along with creole fish and chromis both gray and blue. Tubastrea corals are evident under ledges, and sergeant majors are plentiful, usually seen defending their eggs which resemble purple encrusted areas. Hermit crabs, arrow crabs, and other invertebrates can be turned up for macrophotography enthusiasts.

Typical Depth Range:	10–80 feet
Typical Current Conditions:	Moderate
Expertise Required:	Novice
Access:	Boat

This site is just NNW of Torrens Point and is marked by a large rock formation breaking the surface. The rock at water level is about 100 feet in diameter and rises upwards above the water another 50 feet. Underwater, the terrain is made up of a gray lava sand bottom in 80 feet of water which surrounds the circular reef of outlying mountain peaks and valleys. Barrel sponges are very common on the rock and coral below. Deepwater gorgonians at the base of the rock filter-feed from the currents, capturing their share of

The hawksbill turtle (Eretmochelys imbricata) is often spotted at Diamond Rock. Turtles swim to the surface to breathe, then return underwater for extended swimming periods. (Photo: S. Swygert)

Southern stingrays (Dasyatis americana) use the gray and black sand of Saba for camouflage. The stingray flaps its wings to burrow in the sand for protection. (Photo: J. Schnabel)

the platonic organisms flowing through the sea. Giant orange elephant ear sponges and yellow tube sponges can be seen at this site.

The recommended dive plan here is similar to that of Man O' War Shoals, that is, to circle the reef and slowly ascend along the way for safety, returning to your starting point with a safe margin of air. During calm weather, snorkelers will enjoy the corals and sea life around the circular rock formation.

Encrusting corals like tubastrea, brain coral, fire coral, and star coral have gained a stronghold on the rock. Sea anemones, such as the giant Caribbean and purple anemones, are common among cracks in the rock face. Thick schools of creole fish and gray chromis dance around the reef, filling the scene with motion. Sergeant majors lay their eggs on the wall faces while the coneys and blue tangs seek out the eggs for food.

As the sea floor is flat and sandy, it provides good shelter for southern stingrays, a common sight here. Hawksbill turtles are often seen resting on the rocks for awhile before returning to the surface for air. Rock beauties add colors of yellow and black, complementing the yellow tube sponges. Soldierfish and squirrelfish hide under ledges.

Typical Depth Range:	95–130 feet
Typical Current Conditions:	Moderate
Expertise Required:	Advanced
Access:	Boat

Shark Shoal is located about one mile to the west of Wells Bay and is appropriately named after the blacktip sharks which frequent this site. During the dive briefing, John Magor said he once saw a large bull shark feeding on a school of snapper here. Anything can happen at this site, adding to the exhilaration of a dive at Shark Shoal. The dive plan is to proceed down the mooring line to the seamount; the dive is usually done to a depth of 110 feet for 20 minutes, with a safety stop at 15 feet on the mooring line upon return from your exploration. The pinnacle consists of twin mountain peaks with a valley in between. Yellow tube sponges are heavily entrenched on the wall face, as are orange elephant ear sponges and purple tube sponges. Deepwater gorgonians and tubastrea corals cover undercut ledges.

Caves and undercuts are seemingly etched out of the vertical coral formation, providing good opportunities for the underwater photographer. Schools of Spanish mackerel swirl in and out between the valley areas, creating a silvery vale of reflections. Horse-eye jacks approach, closely eyeing the divers. The mountain peaks are covered with a variety of encrusting hard corals, and wire corals extend in the depths.

Sharks often can be seen in the waters near the pinnacles. (Photo: S. Swygert)

Typical Depth Range:	90–130 feet
Typical Current Conditions:	Moderate
Expertise Required:	Advanced
Access:	Boat

This site, as its name implies, is the most distant pinnacle from shore representing the outer limit to pinnacle or seamount diving on Saba. Outer Limits is located about one mile offshore from Ladder Bay, rising up from 250 feet of water to within 90 feet of the surface. At a depth of 100 feet, the pinnacle is only 100 feet in diameter but widens quickly as it descends to depth.

This dive fits the standard dive profile associated with the pinnacles. Proceed down the mooring line to the seamount; the dive is done to 110 feet for 20 minutes with a safety stop at 15 feet deep for three to five minutes upon return up the mooring line. The dive usually proceeds clockwise from the mooring base, where a sometimes resident yellow frogfish has been seen on a ledge in 90 feet of water. Large orange elephant ear sponges accented by deepwater gorgonians make excellent subjects for wide-angle photography. Return to the mooring for the ascent up the line.

Large schools of creole fish swim through the valley created by cracks in the pinnacle, solitary black jacks appear, and blacktip sharks can be seen in the depths of cobalt blue water. Undercut ledges shelter large tiger groupers and squirrelfish, and wire corals extend out from the wall face. Horse-eye jacks often circle the seamount, and schools of pelagic fish can be seen everywhere in the blue water surrounding the pinnacle.

Amid crevices in the coral, the spotted moray (Gymnothorax moringa) *seeks refuge from predators. (Photo: J. Schnabel)*

Typical Depth Range:	90–130 feet
Typical Current Conditions:	Moderate
Expertise Required:	Advanced
Access:	Boat

Located to the south of the Outer Limits and about one mile west of Ladder Bay, Third Encounter is part of a cluster of pinnacles which ascend from a single connective seamount and include the Twilight Zone, another dive site, to the east. Descending down the mooring, the pinnacle becomes visible before reaching its top at 90 feet deep. The top dips to the west with a vertical protrusion known as "Eye of the Needle," only 50 feet in diameter and rising up from 250 feet deep. The close proximity of the Eye of the Needle makes for an interesting dive plan. Here, divers leave the comfort of the Third Encounter base to swim across blue water to the Eye of the Needle formation. Then they circle the Eye of the Needle and return to the mountaintop prior to ascent up the mooring line. The dive plan is to 110 feet deep for 20 minutes, with a 5-minute safety stop at 15 feet deep upon return up the mooring line. Local divemasters usually ascend slowly up the mooring line, stopping along the way at shallower depths waiting for their dive computers to clear.

The Eye of the Needle is colored by yellow tube sponges, orange elephant ear sponges, deepwater gorgonians, and corals of all varieties. Fish abound everywhere. Thick schools of creole fish, goatfish, horse-eye jacks, schoolmasters, and snappers swim on top of the seamount here. Blacktip sharks can be seen circling off in the blue water. Nurse sharks can be easily spotted sleeping under ledges.

"The Eye of the Needle," illustrated here, is an offshore pinnacle; this painting by Joan Bourque embraces a variety of corals and marine life typical of these types of sites. (Photo: J. Bourque)

Large elephant ear sponges (Agelas clathrodes), shown here at the Third Encounter, are common on the pinnacles. (Photo: J. Schnabel)

4

Diving in St. Eustatius (Statia)

Most all of the diving on St. Eustatius is done just offshore from the seaside capital city of Oranjestad and southward to Kay Bay. The diving is usually conducted from Oranjestad's Lower Town by small boats from Dive Statia (presently the island's only dive operation) to nearby reefs and wrecks. All dives are to fixed depths on flat sand and rock bottoms, with the exception of the wall dive known as the Drop-off at Buccaneer Bay. Several shipwreck sites are less than one-fourth mile offshore from Lower Town in Gallows Bay and make excellent dive sites. Snorkeling is popular along the coastline of Lower Town. Here, you can see the old buildings and warehouses just below the surface and hunt for legal artifacts.

About one-half mile out from Kay Bay, beautiful coral ledges and reefs extend south along the coastline to White Wall at the southern tip of Statia. Several dive sites are located in this area consisting of coral-encrusted ledges and boulders.

Northward in the Jenkins Bay area, a reef system extends in an arc out from shore. This makes for good snorkeling in the shallows and scuba diving in depths of 30 to 50 feet. Here the current usually runs from north to south. Further to the north end of Jenkins Bay, two rocks break the surface and are known locally as Twin Sisters. About 50 yards from the north end of the island, there is an offshore pinnacle which rises up from 70 feet of sand to within 30 feet of the surface. This is an advanced dive, and weather-dependent.

The windward side of the island is seldom dived due to prevailing winds. It is recommended that upon arrival you check in with Dive Statia to seek advice as to the type of dive plan which best suits your needs. Diving in Statia can be done at all levels, but is particularly good for novice and intermediate divers because the depths are usually shallow. As the wrecks have interesting marine life and plentiful fishes, they are particularly good for underwater photography. Dives are usually done as a boat dive at 9:30 a.m. and at 2:00 p.m. Advanced divers will enjoy the Drop-off and exploring the many wrecks. Rental equipment and instruction are available, from resort courses to full certification courses with specialties. For a detailed listing of dive operators, refer to Appendix 1.

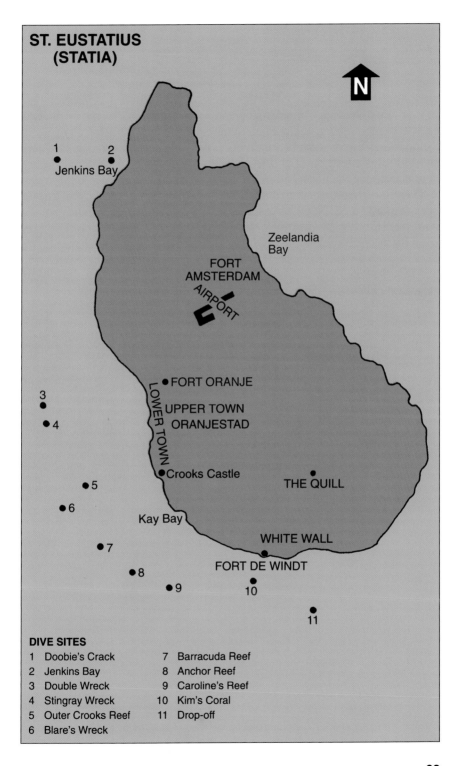

ST. EUSTATIUS (STATIA)

N

1

2
Jenkins Bay

Zeelandia Bay

FORT AMSTERDAM

AIRPORT

3

4

FORT ORANJE

LOWER TOWN

UPPER TOWN

ORANJESTAD

Crooks Castle

THE QUILL

5

6

Kay Bay

WHITE WALL

7

FORT DE WINDT

8

9

10

11

DIVE SITES

1   Doobie's Crack
2   Jenkins Bay
3   Double Wreck
4   Stingray Wreck
5   Outer Crooks Reef
6   Blare's Wreck

7   Barracuda Reef
8   Anchor Reef
9   Caroline's Reef
10 Kim's Coral
11 Drop-off

The Dive Sites

We shall discuss 11 of the more than 15 dive sites on the southern lee coastline of Statia. As diving is difficult and not usually conducted on the windward side, there are no fixed sites there to cover. Dive Statia has placed moorings at key dive sites. As most sites have abundant sand to anchor in, it is easy to explore new areas with no damage to the reef. Access is by boat to the dive sites listed; some beach diving is possible at certain locations. Shore snorkel sites exist, such as the shoreline at Lower Town; small beach entrances along the north end of Lower Town facilitate entry into the water.

There is no marine park to date; although a plan for one exists, it has never been implemented. Nonetheless, the quality of the dive experience is very good because few divers travel through this region. Most of the coral reef sites have large rock ledges with undercut small caves and tunnels to explore with abundant tropical fishes. Exploring the wrecks is interesting and fun; the sand is always shifting so you never know what you will find here. It is estimated that more than 250 ships have met their end in Statian waters, so the possibilities for exploration are endless. The symbol * next to the site name indicates that the site is also good for snorkeling.

*The flamingo tongue shell (*Cyphoma gibbosum*) is a predator of the soft corals. (Photo: J. Schnabel)*

Doobie's Crack 1

Typical Depth Range:	60–100 feet
Typical Current Conditions:	Moderate
Expertise Required:	Advanced
Access:	Boat

Located about one-half mile out from Jenkins Bay, a winding coral ridge runs parallel to shore. One portion of the ridge has a large crevice which extends toward shore. The reef takes its name from a local divemaster who discovered the site years ago. On the deep side, the crevice reaches 100 feet deep and slopes upward to 60 feet deep where there is a plateau of sand. The sand has southern stingrays, razorfish and jawfish. Lobsters line the cuts in the crack; their antennas protrude out for detection of intruders. An occasional blacktip shark circulates through the area, perhaps establishing territorial boundaries or hunting for fish.

The dive plan here usually involves: swimming down the anchor line to the sand plateau below; then swimming down and through Doobie's Crack to a depth of 100 feet; working your way back up the crack to your starting position; and finally returning up the anchor line with a safety stop of five minutes at 15 feet deep.

The spiny lobster (Panulirus argus) *adapts well to its surroundings. Protruding antennas constantly warn of approaching predators. (Photo: J. Schnabel)*

Jenkins Bay * 2

Typical Depth Range:	15–40 feet
Typical Current Conditions:	Light
Expertise Required:	Novice
Access:	Boat

This was once the site of a massive French invasion in 1781 whereby 400 French soldiers surprised British forces on Statia and took the island. Jenkins Bay is probably the most protected dive site on Statia, as the bay arcs inward creating a quiet lagoon good for snorkeling or diving. Large coral-encrusted boulders stretch out for 200 yards close to shore, making an ideal reef for snorkelers to enjoy. The boulders lead out to large patch reef formations ideal for scuba diving.

The coral reefs are surrounded by sandy flats where stingrays congregate. Mountainous star coral, cavernous star coral, boulder coral, sea fans, and small gorgonians make up the reef. Club finger coral clusters are also numerous here.

The bay is almost always calm, providing a good site for beginning scuba divers or neophyte snorkelers. Sand-diver lizardfish peruse the sand flats, while French grunts and yellowtail snappers swim freely throughout the reef system. Careful examination of the coral crevices will turn up a bigeye or two, as well as an occasional flame scallop.

A night dive at this site will often turn up sleeping turtles, slipper lobsters, and hermit crabs.

Diver Kim Brown poses near a large sea fan (Gorgonia ventalina) at Jenkins Bay reef. (Photo: J. Schnabel)

Double Wreck 3

Typical Depth Range:	55–65 feet
Typical Current Conditions:	Light
Expertise Required:	Novice
Access:	Boat

Located about 500 yards northwest of Stingray Wreck are the remains of two 1700s trading ships. Large clumps of ballast stone create a reef system in the middle of a sand bottom. The ballast has formed ridges of coral which shelter numerous schools of French grunts, blackbar soldierfish, and squir-

*Squirrelfish (*Holocentrus rufus*) surround this large basket sponge (*Xestospongia muta*) at Double Wreck. (Photo: J. Schnabel)*

St. Eustatius is one of the few dive destinations where the flying gurnard (Dactylopterus volitans) *can be found easily. (Photo: S. Swygert)*

relfish. Nurse sharks also sleep under these ledges and stingrays burrow in the sand. As these wrecks are spaced out over a sand flat area, they are "the only pub in town" as dive instructor Mike Brown states, creating a "hang-out" for all sorts of marine life. Both the hawksbill and green turtles have been observed at this location.

Schools of margate, snapper, gray chromis, and goatfish teem over the wrecks, adding life to the sunken trading ships. In the sand, lizardfish and flying gurnards swim from one haven to another. Occasionally, splits or cracks appear in the otherwise smooth exterior of the wreck and provide good shelter for lobsters and schools of squirrelfish.

From your anchor position in the sand, follow the wreckage along from clump to clump, marking your return by memory or compass. The wreckage spreads out over some 100 yards of bottom. There is a large, 12-foot anchor on the northeast end of the wreck providing excellent photo opportunities.

Typical Depth Range:	40–55 feet
Typical Current Conditions:	Light
Expertise Required:	Novice
Access:	Boat

Just outside of Dive Statia lies the remains of a late 1700s merchant ship. The wreckage is marked by a ridge with outcroppings of ballast. The ridge shelters soldierfish, squirrelfish, arrow crabs, and banded coral shrimp. Stingrays usually embed themselves in the sand surrounding the wreck. Barrel sponges provide protection for schools of squirrelfish, while flying gurnards can be seen in the sand areas. The dive plan is to follow the anchor line down to the sand bottom in about 45 to 55 feet of water, then work your way around the oval-shaped wreckage area. There is a large anchor located in the center of the reef, which can be used for reference on your return back to the anchor line.

The wreck remains are scattered about the area; sometimes fanning the sand turns up antique bottles and artifacts. Artifacts, however, cannot be removed from the wreck sites. An elevated portion of rock and coral form a ledge area over the wreckage. This is encrusted with brain corals, sea fans, and gorgonians. Seahorses often can be found here with their tails curled around the branches of gorgonians.

Large southern stingrays (Dasyatis americana) congregate in the open expanse of sand surrounding Stingray Wreck. (Photo: J. Schnabel)

Typical Depth Range:	40 feet
Typical Current Conditions:	Light
Expertise Required:	Novice
Access:	Boat

Just outside of Crooks Castle, this reef stretches from shore out to several hundred yards to the south. The area close to shore is ideal for snorkelers. A series of coral ledges make up the reef which shelters myriad tropical fishes among the hard and soft corals. Near the shore, portions of the old Lower Town wall break the surface and form interesting reefs for exploration. Further out in 40 feet of water, a long, low reef parallels the coastline.

Proceed by exploring along the many ledges of the shallow zone, remembering where your starting point is. If your dive is on the outer portion, you will be exploring along the reef parallel to shore. Return to your mooring easily by just turning around and retracing your path. As the depth is a shallow 40 feet, your bottom time will be sufficient to see much of what this site has to offer.

The reef has large barrel sponges, sea fans, and a variety of soft corals. Large schools of French grunts and goatfish swim through the corals; flamingo tongue shells prey on the stalks of gorgonians. Boulder corals and numerous pillar coral stands display their extended polyps during the day. French angelfish and juvenile queen angelfish use this reef for shelter. Coral crabs and spider crabs search the reef for food during the day and night. The sandy areas have lizardfish, flying gurnards, and sand-tile fish, and dusky jawfish peer out from their burrows in the sand.

These smallmouth grunts (Haemulon chrysargyreum) *line the ledges along the low-lying reef at Outer Crooks. (Photo: J. Schnabel)*

Blare's Wreck   6

Typical Depth Range:	60–75 feet
Typical Current Conditions:	Light
Expertise Required:	Intermediate
Access:	Boat

Located about one-half mile out from Crooks Castle, Blare's Wreck takes its name from Wilson Blare, a local fisherman who discovered it. The wreck is mostly below the sand with piles of ballast stone forming a ledge which wraps around the wreckage in a circular fashion. Artifacts, including bottles, china, and metal parts, are often turned up here. Blare's Wreck lies on an area of sand to the north and west and marks the beginning of the coral reef system to the south.

Descend down to the sand bottom in 60 feet of water, follow the ledge around the wreck into the current, return to the mooring site, and ascend up the line with a safety stop of three minutes at 10 feet deep.

Gorgonians and sea fans are in patches to the south of the wreck. The ledge at the wreck rises to 10 feet tall along the north side, and this makes for more interesting exploration.

Large ships' anchors lying partially exposed in the sand often lead divers to new wreck sites on Statia. (Photo: J. Schnabel)

Typical Depth Range: 50–70 feet
Typical Current Conditions: Light
Expertise Required: Intermediate
Access: Boat

Located about one-half mile offshore from Kay Bay is a coral shelf area NNE consisting of a large ledge with undercut caves. The ledge is bordered by sand on the east side. The undercuts shelter large populations of spiny lobsters, and the ledge structure shelters a variety of invertebrates. Banded

Large formations of rock, ballast stone, and wreckage form the foundation for the colorful coral reefs of Statia. (Photo: S. Swygert)

coral shrimp and arrow crabs can be seen among the cracks in the coral, and soldierfish gather in the vertical cuts. From the reef face, the bottom slopes out to the west reaching 90 feet deep before becoming a vertical wall.

The dive plan here is to begin in a northerly direction, exploring the undercut areas in 70 feet of water. There is a large anchor on the north end of the reef that serves as a turn-around point. On your return, explore the upper portion of the reef in 50 feet of water to the mooring, then ascend with a safety stop of three minutes at 15 feet deep. The reef is characterized by large barrel sponges, tall gorgonians, and sea whips. French angelfish, queen angelfish, and schools of goatfish and barracuda frequent this site. The schooling barracudas are always evident here, which accounts for the name of this site. Other fish common to the site are white-spotted filefish, rock beauties, schoolmasters, banded butterflyfish, blue tangs, and trumpetfish.

On the southwest corner of the reef, a large rock formation has deepwater gorgonians and orange and red encrusting sponges.

The damselfish (Eupomacentrus planifrons) *is constantly busy defending its territory. (Photo: S. Swygert)*

Typical Depth Range:	40–70 feet
Typical Current Conditions:	Intermediate
Expertise Required:	Novice
Access:	Boat

The first site south of the Kay Bay area is marked by a large ship's anchor some 14 feet in length on the north end of the reef. The ledges surround a sandy valley area with isolated coral heads. The ledge itself has several grooves which shelter large lobster populations. Both the Caribbean spiny lobster and the Spanish lobster are seen residing within these grooves.

The mooring brings you into a sandy circular area surrounded by a high coral ledge. After descending to the bottom in about 50 feet of water, work your way along the reef to the anchor on the north end. The anchor is heavily encrusted with coral and makes a good photo opportunity. Continue the dive back along the ledge to the mooring, where you may see a stingray in the sand or lobsters in the undercut ledges. Allow enough air for a slow ascent back up the line.

This site has large barrel sponges, large sea fans, and tall gorgonians. A pair of friendly French angelfish can often be seen grazing on sponges and coral encrusted rocks. Trumpetfish take shelter in the gorgonians, waiting for an opportunity to lunge down at unsuspecting damselfish. The queen triggerfish is found here, as are the cowfish and webbed burrfish. Orange elephant ear sponges and deepwater gorgonians grow along the ledge. Orange and red sponges encrust on the underside of the ledge. Yellow tube and vase sponges are common on the topside of the coral ledge.

Wide-angle scenes, complemented by a diver model, provide photo opportunities at Anchor Reef. (Photo: J. Schnabel)

Caroline's Reef 9

Typical Depth Range:	40–60 feet
Typical Current Conditions:	Light
Expertise Required:	Intermediate
Access:	Boat

    This site is located just inside of Anchor Reef toward shore, and is characterized by a sunken sand bottom surrounded by ledges. On top of the ledge is a flat plateau of sea fans and gorgonians. The boat will moor or anchor in the sand between the ledges. After your descent, begin exploration along the west side of the ledge making a slow circle back along the east side to the anchor line. Plan a dive to 60 feet deep for 50 minutes or less. If you explore the upper edge of the reef, do so on the return portion of the dive as it is about 40 to 50 feet deep. In the sand below, an occasional southern

Large clusters of featherdusters (Sabellastarte magnifica) *are a welcome sight for the macrophotographer. (Photo: S. Swygert)*

These encrusting sponges provide shelter for small fishes and invertebrates. (Photo: S. Swygert)

stingray lies, eyes exposed, fanning the sand with its wings. Under the ledges is a heavy covering of encrusting red and orange sponges and some deep-water gorgonians.

Lobsters are seen hiding in cracks in the reef, as are squirrelfish and black-bar soldierfish. Midway through the northwest side of the reef, a small cave extends to the other side of the ledge. This is a particularly good section for wide-angle photo opportunities. Spotted eagle rays can also be sighted swimming through this area.

Many macrophoto opportunities exist here, including a variety of tunicates and featherduster worms, hermit crabs, and nudibranchs. Graysbies and coneys are found on top of the ledge, and French angelfish graze on varieties of sponges here. Parrotfish mark their territories by biting off sections of coral where they patrol regularly, secreting a sandy contribution to the bottom.

A pair of friendly queen angelfish reside here, as do schools of mahogany snappers. Black margates, blue tangs, and surgeonfish swim through, grazing on algae; black durgons are everywhere.

Typical Depth Range:	40 feet
Typical Current Conditions:	Light
Expertise Required:	Novice
Access:	Boat

This site is located about 400 yards from the southwest corner of Statia and is named after instructor Kim Brown who discovered the site. The site appears as a bowl formed by a low, boomerang-shaped ledge on the south side and a circular formation of rocks to the north and west sides surrounding a flat, sandy bottom. Moving around the outside formations, start by exploring into the current, usually clockwise around the bowl in 40 feet of water. This will bring you to the southern ridge which has a slight undercut ledge. The undercuts shelter nurse sharks, squirrelfish, and blackbar soldierfish.

The upper side of the ridge has a variety of sea fans and gorgonians growing atop its surface. Brain coral, mustard hill coral, and finger coral also grow on the ridge surface. French angelfish, rock beauties, and butterflyfish are common to the reef. To the west and north, the rocks and boulders form reefs teeming with fish such as French grunts, goatfish, and yellowtail snappers. Lizardfish, flying gurnards, peacock flounders, and stingrays can be found in the sand within the bowl formation.

Diver Kim Brown poses at Kim's Coral, a site she discovered. (Photo: J. Schnabel)

Typical Depth Range:	60–130 feet
Typical Current Conditions:	Moderate
Expertise Required:	Advanced
Access:	Boat

The Drop-off is located off the south coast of Statia in Buccaneer Bay. The Drop-off begins in about 80 feet of water at the edge of a deep spur and groove system originating in 60 feet of sand to the east of the Drop-off. Here the wall arcs inward towards shore from Anchor Reef and follows the coast toward St. Kitt's.

The profile for this dive is to a depth of 110 feet for 20 minutes, with a safety stop of five minutes at a depth of 15 feet on the anchor line.

The sand bottom in 60 feet of water has many jawfish, razorfish, and sand-tile fish, as well as an occasional stingray. Coral canyons rise up from the grooves of sand which flow out into the Drop-off. The wall face is covered by heavy growths of large deepwater gorgonians and a variety of sponges. An occasional blacktip shark may appear from the depths of the wall to add a little excitement to your dive. Large schools of creole fish and creole wrasses seem to be endlessly transgressing the edge of the Drop-off.

Sea fans, sea whips, and tall gorgonians are intermixed with brain coral, mountain star coral, and other hard coral varieties. Wire coral and black coral extend down the wall to depths of 150 feet or more. Cruising the wall face, you may occasionally encounter spotted eagle rays and horse-eye jacks.

The Drop-off begins in about 80 feet of water at Statia. The wall is alive with color. (Photo: J. Schnabel)

5

Marine Life of St. Maarten, Saba, and St. Eustatius

St. Maarten, Saba, and St. Eustatius are the products of volcanic eruptions which pushed the islands upwards. As time passed, lava entered the sea during eruptions, and boulders were thrown into the sea or broken off during earthquakes. Over the centuries, the lava and broken-off boulders have formed crevices and caves in many areas throughout these islands. Saba is today an inactive volcano, and the offshore seamounts add to the overall mountainous volcanic structure which created the tiny island. The Quill on St. Eustatius also erupted and formed the cone of what is now an inactive volcano, spewing lava into the sea and ejecting boulders which later have become coral reefs.

This similarity between the islands has attracted a cast of thousands of marine mammals, fishes, crustaceans, mollusks, and corals which could adapt to this type of undersea environment. Perhaps the spiny lobster best illustrates a creature which has taken advantage of the many cracks, caves, fissures, and grooves in the rocks and coral to seek refuge.

A sponge decorator crab (Dromidia antillensis) *travels under the camouflage of a sponge carried on its back. (Photo: S. Swygert)*

*The spotted cleaning shrimp (*Periclimenes yucatanicus) *maintains a symbiotic relationship with its host, the giant Caribbean anemone (*Condylactis gigantea). (Photo: S. Swygert)*

The hard and soft corals which grow here provide a natural shelter for the trumpetfish, squirrelfish, and blackbar soldierfish, as well as countless other species. Because there are numerous soft corals, there are numerous flamingo tongue shells which prey on them. The flamingo tongue shell inserts its needle-like proboscis into the cups of the soft coral polyps, removing the live tentacles and leaving a path of destruction in its wake. Grooves in the coral provide niches where the giant Caribbean sea anemone can gain a foothold. Anemone shrimp and cleaning wrasses seek the protection of these anemones. The cleaning shrimp maintains a symbiotic relationship with the anemone. It is immune to the anemone's sting, while attracting small fish which it cleans and which the anemone often consumes. Nudibranchs, particularly the lettuce slug, patrol barren rocks eating algae that grow on them. Arrow crabs and banded coral shrimp are busy cleaning the moray eels. Each of the invertebrates seems to have its own important task which is specially related to the overall health of the coral reef.

Statia is one location where you are almost guaranteed to see the flying gurnard fish which has adapted well to the wide expanse of sand on the island. Disguising itself to match the colors of the sand, when disturbed it fans out colorful wings which change color to match its surroundings and frighten unsuspecting predators. Southern stingrays have evolved to be the perfect species to live in and around the volcanic sand of Statia and Saba. The black or gray sand matches their color identically; when burrowed in the sand, only their eyes are visible, a perfect protection from predation by hungry sharks.

Here in the sand, the stingray flaps its wings, fanning the sand to hunt for crustaceans. The spotted eagle ray, streamlined in design, is an able swimmer that cruises momentarily into sand flats from nearby deep walls to dig up mollusks for food, crushing their shells with its powerful jaws. On Statia, the wrecks create an oasis in the sand, sheltering moray eels, lobsters, crabs, and octopus. Banded coral shrimp and gobies set up cleaning stations near coral heads. A variety of fish take advantage of being cleaned of parasites by the cleaners who receive a meal in return.

The offshore seamounts of Saba, unique in that they are within diveable depths, provide a glance at sea life from a pelagic's viewpoint. Surrounded by large schools of fish which swirl in and out, the seamount provides a moment of protection to those species which might otherwise be hunted in the open sea. Also providing a point of reference in the open sea, the seamount often is a site for mating activities. Blacktip and bull sharks circle the mounts, looking for opportunities to feed on the large schools of fish which congregate there, while the fish in turn seek safety in their large numbers. Manta rays, pilot whales, dolphins, and whale sharks all range through these waters on a seasonal pattern.

As St. Maarten, Saba, and St. Eustatius lie in the Caribbean Sea, they have myriad Caribbean reef fishes. The beautiful queen angelfish, French angelfish, rock beauty, and butterflyfish color the reefs profusely, delighting the snorkelers and divers who are fortunate enough to experience these waters. The spectacular reefs and the variety of diving possibilities make the three islands an ideal diving destination. Above water, the beauty and history of the islands is astounding; underwater, you will find your curiosity piqued and knowledge challenged to understand the mysteries of the Caribbean Sea.

The longsnout seahorse (Hippocampus reidi) usually seeks shelter amid the soft corals. This predominantly white specimen is a rare sight. (Photo: J. Magor)

6

Safety

Diving in St. Maarten, Saba, and St. Eustatius is usually quite safe. As most all diving is done by boats, you will be diving with experienced dive guides. All dives should be carefully planned because they will usually be made to fixed depths for fixed periods of time, with safety stops a recommended practice. Use of the dive tables will require close attention to your time and depth. Use of dive meters will require not pushing the meters to their limits. Whether using the tables or dive meters, it's always a good idea to build in safety factors.

The safe limit for sport diving is 130 feet; dives in these islands will be to depths less than this limit. Select a guided dive until you feel comfortable with your environment. Remember, you can always learn more from local divemasters about the diving in their region. Plan your dives to turn around and head back to your boat at 1,500 psi or more. Navigate carefully—do not leave the area of the boat until you have planned your return and mem-

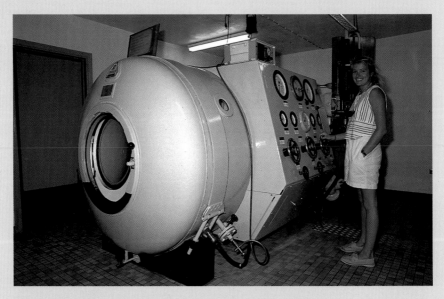

Saba Marine Park manager Susan Walker White oversees chamber operation at Fort Bay, Saba. (Photo: J. Schnabel)

orized the terrain. Get lots of sleep, don't drink alcohol, and drink plenty of fluids to avoid dehydration.

Divers should be aware of some of the possible discomforts which could be caused by careless misinterpretation of their underwater surroundings. Because the formations in these islands are rocky in nature, they provide homes for scorpionfish who can camouflage themselves to look like rocks. They do this so that when bite-sized fish swim past, they can leap up and instantly swallow their dinner. If you were to step or put your hand down on one of their dorsal spines, they could penetrate your skin and inject a venomous toxin. The resulting sting requires immediate medical attention, as it will be quite painful and damage the tissue in the area of the puncture wound.

Fire coral is described as being a light, mustard-colored coral covered with stinging hair-like nematocysts. Contact between this coral and your bare skin will cause painful red welts. Fire coral is in three varieties: leafy fire coral, blade-like coral, and encrusting fire coral. Relief from the sting will be aided by using a Benadryl cream on the affected area.

Proper buoyancy techniques and good diving practices will minimize your contact with delicate corals, preserving the corals and preventing damage to you at the same time. For assistance with buoyancy control techniques, seek the help of a local diving instructor.

A master of disguise, the scorpionfish (Scorpaena plumieri) imitates a rock. The venomous dorsal spines can inflict pain and injury if touched. (Photo: J. Schnabel)

Attaching themselves to soft coral branches or crawling over hard corals, bristle worms can be injurious to unsuspecting divers. Their appearance is like that of a caterpillar with a red body and white bristles. The bristles cause a painful sting when touched. Treatment requires removing the bristles with tape or tweezers and applying antihistamine spray like Benadryl to stop swelling and relieve pain.

Nightdivers should be aware of a box-like, transparent jellyfish with tentacles trailing from each of its four corners. This is the sea wasp, so named because it inflicts a wasp-like but more severe sting when touched. The sting is very painful and may require ice and oral Benadryl. Persons suffering allergic reaction (anaphylactic shock) will require immediate medical attention, which usually involves Benadryl injections or Epinephrine IV. The Portuguese man-of-war is another jellyfish worth mentioning here. While not usually a problem in these waters, its territory does include these islands. The jellyfish resembles a purple balloon-like float suspended at the surface with stinging tentacles dangling below. Contact with the tentacles causes severe pain. Treatment is to remove the tentacles without touching them; treat the same as with the sea wasp sting.

Reaching your fingers back into holes or crevices is not recommended, as divers have suffered moray bites doing this. The bite is lacerating, causing bleeding and pain. Stop bleeding with pressure, clean, and apply antibiotic cream. Seek medical assistance, as the bite may require oral antibiotics. Feeding the fish and eels is not recommended; not only does this alter their natural feeding habits, it invites bothersome bites as well.

The Saba Marine Park maintains a four-place recompression chamber at Fort Bay, Saba, and is the main facility serving St. Maarten, Saba, and St. Eustatius. The telephone number is 05-3295 locally; overseas, call (011) 599-5-3295. Do not call unless in an emergency.

DAN: The Divers Alert Network, a membership association of individuals and organizations sharing a common interest in diving safety, operates a 24-hour national hotline, (919) 684-8111 (collect calls are accepted in an emergency). DAN does not directly provide medical care; however, it does provide advice on early treatment, evacuation, and hyperbaric treatment of diving-related injuries. Additionally, DAN provides diving safety information to members to help prevent accidents. Membership is $10 a year, offering: the DAN *Underwater Diving Accident Manual* describing symptoms and first-aid for major diving-related injuries; emergency room physician guidelines for drugs and IV fluids; a membership card listing diving-related symptoms on one side and DAN's emergency and non-emergency phone numbers on the other; one tank decal and three small equipment decals with DAN's logo and emergency number; and a newsletter, *Alert Diver,* which describes diving medicine and provides safety information in layman's language and includes articles for professionals, case histories, and questions related to diving. Special memberships to dive stores, dive clubs, and corporations are also available. The *DAN Manual* can be purchased for $4 from the Administrative Coordinator, National Diving Alert Network, Duke University Medical Center, Box 3823, Durham, NC 27710.

DAN divides the U.S. into seven regions, each coordinated by a specialist in diving medicine who has access to the hyperbaric chambers in his region. Non-emergency or information calls are connected to the DAN office and information number, (919) 684-2948. This number can be dialed direct, Monday through Friday between 9 a.m. and 5 p.m. EST. Divers should not call DAN for general information on chamber locations. Chamber status changes frequently, making this kind of information dangerous if obsolete at the time of an emergency. Instead, divers should contact DAN as soon as a diving emergency is suspected to confirm the location of the nearest chamber. All divers should have comprehensive medical insurance and check to make sure that hyperbaric treatment and air ambulance are covered internationally.

Diving is a safe sport, and there are very few accidents compared to the number of divers and number of dives made each year. But when the infrequent injury does occur, DAN is ready to help. DAN, originally 100% federally funded, is now largely supported by the diving public. Membership in DAN or purchase of DAN manuals or decals provides divers with useful safety information and provides DAN with necessary operating funds. Donations are tax-deductible, as DAN is a legal, non-profit public service organization.

Avoid touching the colorful bristle worm (Hermodice cananculata)*; the bristles cause severe pain and burning. (Photo: S. Swygert)*

Appendix 1: Dive Operators

The list below is included as a service to the reader. The authors have made every effort to make this list complete at the time the book was printed. This list does not necessarily constitute an endorsement of these businesses.

St. Maarten

Dutch Side

Pelican Watersports and Dive Center
P.O. Box 3012 Simpson Bay
St. Maarten, Neth. Antilles
Tel./Fax 011 599-5-42640

Tradewinds Dive Center
Great Bay Marina, Philipsburg
St. Maarten, Neth. Antilles
Tel. 011 599-5-24096

Ocean Explorers Dive Center
Simpson Bay
St. Maarten, Neth. Antilles
Tel./Fax 011 599-5-45252

Caribbean Explorer
(Live-aboard dive boats)
P.O. Box 310
Mills, WY 82644
Tel. 1-800-322-3577
Fax 307-235-0686

Leeward Island Divers
Simpson Bay Yacht Club
Airport Road
St. Maarten, Neth. Antilles
Tel. 011 599-5-42866
Fax 011 599-5-42262

French Side

Blue Ocean Dive Center
La Belle Creole Hotel
Baie Nettle, Marigot
St. Martin, F.W.I.
Tel. 011 590 87-89-73
Fax 011 590 87-26-36

Lou's Scuba Club
La Marine Hotel
Baie Nettle, Marigot
St. Martin, F.W.I.
Fax 011 590-87-20-14

Saba

Sea Saba Dive Center
P.O. Box 530
Windwardside
Saba, Neth. Antilles
Tel. 011 599-4-62246
Fax 011 599-4-62362

Saba Deep Scuba Center
P.O. Box 22
Fort Bay
Saba, Neth. Antilles
Tel. 011 599-4-63347
Fax 011 599-4-63397

Wilson's Dive Shop
Fort Bay
Saba, Neth. Antilles
Tel./Fax 011 599-4-62541

Saba Marine Park—Fort Bay

Susan Walker White
P.O. Box 18, The Bottom
Saba, Neth. Antilles
Tel. 011 599-4-63295
Fax 011 599-4-63435

St. Eustatius

Dive Statia
P. O. Box 158 Oranjestad
St. Eustatius, Neth. Antilles
Tel. 011 599-3-82435
Fax 011 599-3-82539

Diving activities take place close to shore on St. Eustatius. The Quill, an extinct volcano, is visible in the background. (Photo: J. Schnabel)

Appendix 2: Hotels and Accommodations

The list below is included as a service to the reader. The authors have made every effort to make this list complete at the time the book was printed. This list does not necessarily constitute an endorsement of these businesses.

St. Maarten

Dutch Side

Great Bay Beach Hotel
P.O. Box 310 Philipsburg
St. Maarten, Neth. Antilles
Tel. 011 599-5-22446
Fax 011 599-5-23859

Belair Suites Beach Hotel
Welgelegen Road, Cay Hill
P.O. Box 140
St. Maarten, Neth. Antilles
Tel. 011 599-5-23362
Fax 011 599-5-25295

Divi Little Bay Beach Hotel
St. Maarten, Neth. Antilles
Tel. 607 277-3484
Fax 607 277-3624

La Vista Hotel
P.O. Box 40 Pelican Key
St. Maarten, Neth. Antilles
Tel. 011 599-5-43005
Fax 011 599-5-43010

Port De Plaisance
P.O. Box 2089 Cole Bay
St. Maarten, Neth. Antilles
Tel. 011 599-5-45222
Fax 011 599-5-42428

Holland House Beach Hotel
P.O. Box 393 Philipsburg
St. Maarten, Neth. Antilles
Tel. 011 599-5-22572
Fax 011 599-5-24673

The Oyster Pond Hotel
P.O. Box 239 Oyster Pond
St. Maarten, Neth. Antilles
Tel. 011 599-5-22206
Fax 011 599-5-25695

Maho Beach Hotel
Maho Bay
St. Maarten, Neth. Antilles
Tel. 011 599-5-52115
Fax 011 599-5-53180

Pelican Resort
P.O. Box 431 Simpson Bay
St. Maarten, Neth. Antilles
Tel./Fax 011 599-5-42503

Royal Palm Beach Club
P.O. Box 431 Simpson Bay
St. Maarten, Neth. Antilles
Tel./Fax 011 599-5-42503

Royal Islander Club, La Plage
P.O. Box 2000 Maho Reef
St. Maarten, Neth. Antilles
Tel. 011 599-5-52505
Fax 011 599-5-52585

The Towers at Mullet Bay
P.O. Box 2024 Mullet Bay
St. Maarten, Neth. Antilles
Tel. 011 599-5-53069
Fax 011 599-5-53074

Sea Breeze Hotel
Welgelegen Rd. Cay Hill
St. Maarten, Neth. Antilles
Tel. 011 599-5-26054
Fax 011 599-5-26057

French Side

Anse Margot
B P 979—Baie Nettle
St. Martin, F.W.I.
Tel. 87-92-01
Fax 87-92-13

Chez Martine
BP 637—Grand Case
St. Martin, F.W.I.
Tel. 87-51-59
Fax 87-87-30

Grand Case Beach Club
Grand Case
St. Martin, F.W.I.
Tel. 87-51-87
Fax 87-59-93

Hotel Mont Vernon
BP 1174—Chevrise
St. Martin, F.W.I.
Tel. 87-42-22
Fax 87-37-27

La Samana
BP 576—Terres Basses
St. Martin, F.W.I.
Tel. 87-51-22
Fax 87-87-86

Captain Oliver's
BP 645—Oyster Pond
St. Martin, F.W.I.
Tel. 87-40-26
Fax 87-40-84

Esmeralda Resort
BP 541—Baie Orientale
St. Martin, F.W.I.
Tel. 87-36-36
Fax 87-35-18

Hevea
Grand Case
St. Martin, F.W.I.
Tel. 87-56-85
Fax 87-83-88

La Belle Creole
BP—Baie Nettle
St. Martin, F.W.I.
Tel. 87-58-66
Fax 87-56-66

Le Jardins De Chevrise
Mont Vernon
St. Martin, F.W.I.
Tel./Fax 87-38-03

Le Meridien L'Habitation
BP 581—Anse Marcel
St. Martin, F.W.I.
Tel. 87-33-33
Fax 87-30-38

Marina Royale
BP 176—Marigot
St. Martin, F.W.I.
Tel. 87-52-46
Fax 87-92-88

Marine Hotel Simson Beach
BP 172—Baie Nettle
St. Martin, F.W.I.
Tel. 87-54-54
Fax 87-92-11

Saba

Captain's Quarters
P.O. Box 17
Saba, Neth. Antilles
Tel. 011 599-4-62299
800-365-8484

Juliana's
Windwardside
Saba, Neth. Antilles
Tel. 800-365-8484
     011 599-4-62269

Scout's Place
Windwardside
Saba, Neth. Antilles
Tel. 011 599-4-62205

Cranston's Antique Inn
The Bottom
Saba, Neth. Antilles
Tel. 011 599-4-63216

For more listings contact . . .

Saba Real Estate N.V.
P.O. Box 17
Saba, Neth. Antilles
Tel. 011 599-4-62299

Saba Tourist Bureau
Windwardside
Saba, Neth. Antilles
Tel. 011 599-4-62231
Fax 011 599-4-63274

Saba Info. Office
271 Main St.
Northport, NY 11768
Tel. 800 344-4606
Fax 516 261-9606

St. Eustatius

The Old Gin House
P.O. Box 172
St. Eustatius, Neth. Antilles
Tel. 011 599-3-82319

The Golden Era
Lower Town
St. Eustatius, Neth. Antilles
Tel. 011 599-3-82345
800-365-8484
Fax 011 599-3-83445

Talk of the Town
L.E. Saddlerweg
St. Eustatius, Neth. Antilles
Tel./Fax 011 599-3-82236
Tel. 800-365-8484

La Maison Sur La Plage
Zeelandia Bay
St. Eustatius, Neth. Antilles
Tel. 011 599-3-82256

Henriquez Apts.
Tel. 011 599-3-82299

Alvin Courtar Apts
Tel. 011 599-3-82218

Lens Apts.
Tel. 011 599-3-82226

Juria Cottage
Tel. 011 599-3-82291

Richardson Guest House
Tel. 011 599-3-82378

Sugar Hill Apts.
Tel. 011 599-3-82305

Airport View Apts.
Tel. 011 599-3-82474

For more listings, contact . . .

The St. Eustatius Dept. of Tourism
Oranjestad
St. Eustatius, Neth. Antilles
Tel. 011 599-3-82433
Fax 011 599-3-82324

Index

Boldface page numbers indicate illustrations.